A Gift Of Wonder

A GIFT OF WONDER

A True Story Showing School as It Should Be

KIM ALLSUP

Lindisfarne | 2017

*The publication of this book was made possible
by a grant from the Waldorf Curriculum Fund.*

Published by Lindisfarne Books
an imprint of SteinerBooks *Anthroposophic Press, Inc.*
www.steinerbooks.org
610 Main Street, Great Barrington, Massachusetts 01230

ISBN: 978-1-58420-954-6
e-book ISBN: 978-1-58420-955-3

Contents

REFLECTIONS

For Geoff

and for partners and supporters of teachers everywhere

Foreword

IF YOU PICKED UP THIS BOOK to read a great story, please skip this foreword and go straight to the substance of the book itself. However, if you are a reader interested in considering how classroom experience relates to the future of schooling, this foreword might be helpful in comprehending the importance of the book as an entire, artistic statement about the urgent need to find a fresh approach to educating our youth, our future.

Wonder is a challenging word. It has been overused and commercialized and its true definition endangered. In the face of that risk, Kim Allsup's straightforward courage in titling her book *A Gift of Wonder* is commendable.

Wonder is a uniquely human experience, and used as a means to an end in sales and advertising distracts us from its highest value as an end in itself. To never give up on the essence of such an important word carries us forward as a culture, and the story in this book holds the potential for reclaiming the word for its essential meaning.

This book is more than a simple "story of my life." Recounting specific experiences teaching at a small Waldorf school on Cape Cod, and the life events that got her there, Allsup develops the mood and after-images of her book in a way that weaves an unusually lovely cloak for us to see—rather, a magic cloak that gives us a new perception of childhood, teaching, and education.

Allsup is drawn to Waldorf teacher training because of its focus on wonder—teaching out of wonder and toward wonder. This focus on wonder is unique to Waldorf schools. "The point" of education in our world is, increasingly, performance, bottom lines, and specific information. Good teachers everywhere know the value of wonder but are forced more and more into putting this wonder into service toward a specific end. Wonder is never a goal in itself as an attitude towards life and learning. More's the pity, since it is clear from All-sup's story that an inner habit of wonder makes us life-long learn-ers. Her own discoveries about the meaning of her teacher-training course work, and her unriddling of the personalities of and motiva-tors for the children in her class become the weft for the weave of her life. She describes with power the discipline of waiting, of uncovering, of allowing the designs in children and in their social interactions to develop meanings and illuminations of their own.

This idea of an eight-year journey with a single class teacher (rounded out with language teachers, handwork teachers, music teachers, and others) in Waldorf schools is controversial. Fueled with strained memories of teachers from their own childhood, modern thinkers balk at the possibility of a single teacher guiding the project of elementary and middle school years. But this book illuminates the effectiveness of many years together with a single teacher and a basic assemblage of students.

In an interesting twist of fate, Allsup makes this point through the story of a teacher who is unable to complete the whole eight-year cycle. The ponderings and pain this causes the teacher (pressed by life circumstances) and the thundering strength of the eight year commitment—longer than many jobs, longer than many marriag-es—are made clear in the completion of only six. Though the point is made that eight years together is fulfilling as an ideal, it is never discussed directly. It rises up as the negative space around the story. Allsup's realization that the journey must come to an end prematurely emerges unexpectedly, and we as readers are left to wonder at this. What promises can last this long? What can the connection between student and teacher mean to children, young people, learning about their world and the relationships of the people in it? The story leaves us with resounding answers to these questions in the weaving of the life we are experiencing through this book.

Today there are many questions about education. Technology, with all its own wonders and answers, has left us believing that information might be the same thing as education, that teachers are less and less necessary as children are taught to look up the answers to all questions with a phone or a computer. And yet, even as those in the fields of technology invent smaller and more powerful machines to answer questions, the questions of a satisfying life seem to increase, not decrease.

Kim Allsup's weaving of her journey as a Waldorf teacher with her class, and the path of her life that led her to it, leaves the after-image of how the most important threads in any child's life, in every child's education, are in the hearts and hands of the child's teachers. There is no beautiful tapestry possible with only the threads of information. The insights of teachers who can see each child and who he or she might become are essential. Teachers like Allsup who are determined to allow young people to discover as they wonder on their own are helpful teachers. These are the teachers who can insist that students rise to their own heights simply because they work to see those heights. A teacher who can cultivate an inner habit of wonder can then gather these threads and offer them to every individual to make a wonderful, complex tapestry of each life.

This is the gift of wonder, in the end, of this well-told tale.

Patrice Maynard
San Miguel, Mexico; 2016

Introduction

If I had influence with the good fairy who is supposed to preside over the christen-
ing of all children, I should ask that her gift to each child in the world be a sense of
wonder so indestructible that it would last throughout life, as an unfailing antidote
to boredom and disenchantments of later years, the sterile preoccupation with things
that are artificial, the alienation from the sources of our strength.

—Rachel Carson

There was a time when meadow, grove, and stream,
The earth, and every common sight,
To me did seem
Appareled in celestial light,
The glory and the freshness of a dream.

—William Wordsworth

EVEN AS AN EIGHT-YEAR-OLD CHILD, I was allowed to explore the
beach alone. Far up the hill my mother watched me through a window, but I was not aware of her presence. Walking in salty, knee-
deep water along the sixty-foot sandy stretch between the earthen
dock and the eelgrass, I did not know about the formal study of eco-
systems or habitats, but I marveled at how the periwinkles and the
hermit crabs had their favored areas. I stroked slippery jellyfish that
undulated around my knees and scratchy starfish, which preferred to
grip the rocks under the dock. I examined mussels in tightly bunched
clusters amid the razor-edged eelgrass and knew that horseshoe crabs
had crawled up the sand to deposit the green clusters of transparent
eggs that I accidentally unearthed when digging in the upper beach.
Not all creatures received my benign interest. When hungry I would
wriggle my bare toes in the muddy ooze to unearth fist-sized quahogs

and then imitate a seagull by throwing my hardbound treasure onto a boulder so I could pry open the cracked shell and slurp it up raw.

Here, at the beach, and in a nearby, glorious, old apple tree, I experienced the condition of wonder that is the natural habitat of childhood. I remember spring afternoons, perched in the uppermost limbs looking out beyond the beach to the tide-swollen river, drunk with the scent of apple blossoms, speaking extemporaneous poetry about the beauty around me. (How I wish for a fairy's transcription of those childhood verses.)

The school year brought our family away from the saltwater estuary to a suburban neighborhood where a shallow, freshwater river with a stonewall embankment, flanked by a strip of forest, provided a fairyland for my best friend and me. In our imaginations we transformed the woodland path into a wonderland. Here, healing fairies lived in the hollows of trees, witches peered out from the briar patch, and invisible companions accompanied us on our adventures.

But, during the school year, not all playtime was in a magical grove. The playground at school consisted of a metal swing set and monkey bars on an expanse of sand and gravel pounded into a concrete-like substance where nothing grew. Playing in this lifeless zone, I was aware of my yearning for soft grass, for scuffling through fallen leaves, for flowers and butterflies.

In spite of this barren playground, school was a place where I found wonder. One day my third grade teacher, Mrs. Bromley, called me to her desk and handed me a thick book, *Little House in the Big Woods*, by Laura Ingalls Wilder. "I think you could read this," she said in a soft voice. Perhaps she was attempting to stop the incessant yo-yoing from my desk to the bookshelf then back to my desk in an insatiable search for yet another short picture book that I had not already read. Perhaps she knew that it was time to show me that I was ready to open an unseen door.

I carried the heavy, hardbound book to my desk, sat down and did not get up for a long time. The room disappeared and I was swept away to the Ingalls' log cabin in Wisconsin where the woods went on as far as a man could walk in a month and still see nothing but forest, where the trees whispered together and the wolves howled at night. After many minutes, I looked up and discovered that nobody seemed to mind that I had gone to the Ingalls homestead in the wilderness. Moving deeper into Laura's story, I felt on a deep, unspeakable level that I was moving into a new chapter in my life, that entering the big woods was just the beginning. I was amazed by so many new things all at once, by my ability to keep reading in a book that did not end after twenty pages, by the enchantment of a complex, believable world between two book covers, by the dimly realized expectation that there would be more chapter books and that I was embarking on an auspicious journey. I could not have said all of this, but I felt all of it as the pathway opened into the big woods and many lands beyond.

It is that feeling of wonder, that sense of awe and expectation, of being pulled inextricably into something marvelous, interesting, beautiful, amazing, and compelling that should be the underpinning, the foundation, the living roots of every person's experience of the world as they enter it through a series of stages during childhood.

It is impossible to underestimate the value of wonder in child-hood. It is the mother's milk of the soul, the human foundation for a lifelong worldview that affirms our joyful existence in the web of life. When we experience the condition of awe called wonder, we are lured outside ourselves and the soul is stretched and is irresistibly drawn to become one with a piece of the universe previously outside of our awareness. Our inner self connects pleasurably with what we saw as outside and draws it in. Through the experience of wonder, something new takes root within our very being, and learning begins.

If we encounter this experience often enough, or are fortunate to live in a state of wonder for much of our childhood, we become optimistic and learn to seek that which amazes in every aspect of our lives. A sense of wonder is a primary pathway for learning; it kindles love for nature and for humanity, inspires work, and, if the time and condition for wonder is regular, develops the sense of reverence that underlies spirituality.

The ability and inclination to approach the world with a sense of wonder is inborn, or, as Rachel Carson suggested, "the gift of the good fairy." The gift of eyesight allows us to appreciate a sunset, to read a book, to walk through the forest, and to paint a picture. So too, the gift of wonder is an innate capacity that helps us appreciate the world around us, to understand it, to find our way through it and to create our own original contributions. Parents and teachers cannot give this gift, but they can recognize it in each child and can draw it out. In fact, one of the Latin roots of the word education is *educere*, which means to draw out or to draw forth. School should be a habitat for wonder, a veritable ecosystem for awe and amazement, and teachers should be trained to nurture wonder in their students.

Parents have a special role in kindling wonder and some of the deepest joys of parenting arise while sharing moments of wonder with children. While school life is limited by fixed schedules, life outside of school includes weekends and vacations when families can enjoy long stretches of time in nature, the most powerful source of wonder. A family trip to the beach, or the child's solo foray into the neighborhood woods, can give rise to the quiet, contemplative experience of wonder that I remember from my childhood. At the same time, school offers a different path to wonder that can be less accessible at home. Conversations among students of similar ages allow children to help each other explore questions that arise from their common worldview. This story shares many such conversations.

Kelly Bulkeley, author of *The Wondering Brain*, writes, "Wonder, as I will employ the term, is the feeling excited by an encounter with something novel and unexpected, something that strikes a person as intensely real, true and/or beautiful." For children, so much of daily life is new. If the offerings of parents and teachers and their own encounters in the natural world are beautiful or significant to the child, his or her experience of an ever-evolving symphony of wonder can be almost continuous. Adults who live in a close relationship with children have the privilege of witnessing a continuous revelation of understanding tinged with awe. Watching a child growing in this way can match the intensity of our own childhood amazement.

A vital aspect of the work of parents and teachers involves purposely supporting a general background mood of wonder by surrounding children with beauty, meaning, and truth. To this end, teachers can create lessons that we hope will inspire. Parents can create a home life that includes an unhurried schedule with free time outside, exposure to and participation in live music, visits to the library, trips to forests, gardens, beaches, and mountains. But, even this is not enough; no school curriculum can completely script wonder and even the most inspired home life can increase, but not guarantee, moments of jaw-dropping, wide-eyed awe. The most intense moments of wonder at school often arise unexpectedly in a child or in a class as a whole. Similarly, the opening to an amazing conversation with parents may not happen during a forest hike, but rather on the congested highway during the ride home while the parents had the sense to leave the radio off. In the end it is good to have a plan, but it is important to be willing to throw it away when a child asks an unexpected question, makes an intriguing observation, or stops in awed silence.

We know we are on the right path as teachers and as parents when we are surprised to see wonder emerging when we least expect it. During these moments, we must stop and accord this primal gesture of mind and heart due regard. Teachers put the planned lesson on hold, and parents postpone bedtimes or cleaning the garage to allow for a journey into uncharted territory. The art of teaching and the art of parenting rely on an intuitive dance that moves between honoring our plans and supporting unexpected explorations initiated by a child's curiosity, interest, or wonder.

The public library was the wonderland of my high school years. I often settled at a table near the poetry section where I found inspiration from Whitman, Ferlingetti and Ginsberg. Then, one day, grazing through non-fiction titles, I discovered a book by psychologist Abraham Maslow. Discovering *Toward a Psychology of Being* became my high school equivalent of finding *Little House in the Big Woods*. Learning about Maslow's theories, I felt on a deep, unspeakable level that I was moving into a new chapter in my life. His descriptions of motivation in healthy people lured me away from the beat poets and from my homework and onto the path that would eventually lead me to become a psychology major in college.

Maslow identified two types of motivation, deficiency motivation and growth motivation. People who lack basic physical and emotional fulfillment supplied by breathing, nutrition, safety, belongingness, and self-esteem, experience deficiency motivation as they attempt to replace what is missing. In contrast, people whose basic needs have been met are freed from worry about where their next meal will come from or whether they are worthy of approval. They are motivated instead by the mysterious forces of growth that exist in every organism. These forces cause a blade of grass to shoot toward the sun, cause a baby to stand and walk, and propel children to learn fueled by wonder and curiosity.

Maslow found that individuals with vibrant psychological health had a tendency toward "peak experiences," moments in which a sense of wonder is combined with deep peace and tranquility, a sense of harmony and oneness with the universe. He focused on adult motivation, but I think that his description of human motivation applies to children as well. When children's basic needs are met, it is possible for them to ascend to the highest levels of psychological health, to have peak experiences, possibly while swishing through a tidal estuary, sitting atop a flowering apple tree, participating in an intense conversation in class, or being immersed in a book.

As parents and teachers we have much to gain and nothing to lose when we learn to lift ourselves and our children into growth motivation while steering clear of deficiency motivation. Unfortunately, we live in a culture where children are taught to live in a state of deficiency motivation from an early age. Where we go wrong relates to the ways in which parents and teachers attempt to support healthy confidence. Maslow identifies self-esteem as a lower order need that must be satisfied as part of the journey to full psychological health. As such, self-esteem should be a guaranteed right of each child, in the same way we provide food and water. I think parents and teachers know this instinctively, for increasingly they tend to flood children with praise in the hope that this constant support will instill deep and abiding self-confidence. This is a big mistake based on an understandable misunderstanding.

Authentic, unshakable self-confidence is rooted in real accomplishment and in seeing ones own achievements. Children need frequent opportunities to sing, play a musical instrument, make a potholder, knit a scarf, draw a picture, model with clay, to work in a garden. They need to work at all of this with support from adults who avoid distracting the child with too much direction or with effusive praise. This forbearance on the part of adults allows the child's own fragile sensibilities to emerge. The quiet that surrounds their efforts allows the child to focus on the activity rather than be concerned about their level of achievement. The deep focus that results makes an opening for the child to experience joy when noticing a seedling uncurling from the soil, satisfaction in creating harmony in music, and beauty in blending colors in a painting. Ultimately, discovering a sense of personal, uncoached satisfaction in work leads a child to become intrinsically motivated to work and to learn.

During the first seventy years of the twentieth century, visitors to Yellowstone Park were allowed to feed the bears. Bear related traffic jams were common in the park as were human and bear interactions that did not always turn out well for the humans or the bears. Today "bear jams," injuries, and property damage are almost non-existent because trash cans in the park are bear proof and people are no longer allowed to feed the bears. As the bears returned to finding their own food they tended to move away from areas of human habitation, back to the places in the ecosystem that had supported them for thousands of years.

Praising children too often creates dynamics similar to those that develop by feeding wildlife. The child whose self-confidence becomes dependent on praise and good grades loses the ability to discover a sense of accomplishment on her own and becomes dependent on and oriented toward approval by others. Just as the bears lost their place in the ecosystem, so over-praised children wander away from natural supports to learning—wonder, curiosity, personal initiative, self-propelled, hard work, and a self-conferred sense of accomplishment.

The over-praised child soon realizes that the adults who give rewards can also take them away. When a child becomes anxious about the reactions of parents and teachers, a fragile sense of self-esteem develops and deficiency motivation takes over. The child develops a hole that can never be filled, a mindset for a future plagued by anxiety.

Grounding in authentic self-esteem and a mood of wonder provides a necessary foundation for the healthy growth of the inner life of the grade school child. The mood of innocent wonder helps children practice attention and leads to a capacity for gratitude. Curiosity grows out of wonder and becomes increasingly sophisticated as it evolves into an ability to carry out sustained inquiry. When children live in wonder, gratitude, and curiosity, they practice non-judgmental observation and attention. Secure in self-built confidence, they are free from worry about recognition and are able to connect deeply with the significant people in their lives. This habit of attentive openness develops into compassion and commitment.

I have no doubt that the wonder I experienced along the two rivers of my childhood led me to my first career. I still remember reading the advertisement for an intern at an ecology organization and feeling my heart quicken in the hope that I could do something to protect the worlds of wonder I had known as a child.

I became a specialist in organizing public involvement in environmental decision-making. Most of my work was in a city office, far from the rivers I vowed to protect. Yet, my memory of childhood wonder was never far from my mind. Once, I organized a workshop where participants were asked why working to protect their local estuary was important to them. I was surprised by heartfelt stories of childhood enchantment at the seashore that poured forth not only

from environmental activists, but also scientists, government planners, shellfishermen, and politicians. Similar childhood experiences
had motivated many different modes of commitment. A drop of
wonder can inspire an ocean of work.

I launched my second career, as a teacher, after witnessing joy in
learning during our daughter's first five years at the Waldorf School
of Cape Cod, where the mission statement says, "We cultivate in the
children a feeling of wonder, reverence for life, and respect for self
and others...." Here, kindergarten playthings were shells, stones, wool,
handmade toys and dolls, and the playground looked out over a saltwater pond. The wonder did not stop in the playground nor did the
wonder years end in pre-school.

I began teaching at forty years of age at this young school after it
had moved to an old sea captain's home that parents and teachers had
transformed into a cozy schoolhouse. I had only seven children in my
first grade classroom, a room that had served as a small bedroom for
almost a century. The following year, I stayed with the same group of
children, now second graders, and our growing school moved into a
big brick edifice, an antique school building atop a gentle rise within
sight of the ships that ply the Cape Cod Canal. Our new classroom
was four times as large as the modified bedroom. It had high ceilings, real slate blackboards and three of its five enormous windows
looked down the long grassy slope of the recess field. Here, I shepherded eighteen students, for I had agreed to teach a combined class
that consisted of my original students and the new first grade class.
Each year after that, for the next five years, we moved up the grades
together, this group of children and I, until my combined class was
made up of fifth and sixth grade students. At the end of that year, an
illness in our family led us to move one hundred miles away to the
hill country of southern New Hampshire. Had I not been compelled

to leave my class, I would have completed my intended journey with them three years later with the graduation of the younger group in eighth grade. Our school did not invent the tradition of making class teachers responsible for a group of students from age six, just out of kindergarten, until they are fourteen, on the brink of high school. Nor did we come up with the idea that education should help children to become intrinsically motivated rather than driven by fear of failure or the promise of external rewards. We inherited many traditions, practices and methods when the parents in our fledgling school chose to become part of the worldwide Waldorf movement, which had been in existence since 1919 and now includes more than one thousand independent Waldorf schools in sixty countries. Working in a school where a teacher leads a group of children through the landscape of childhood gave me the opportunity to make observations that I hope will be of use to both teachers and parents.

I was fortunate to grow up in the middle years of the twentieth century, a time when a child could be lost in reading without concern about being tested on the story, when a young girl could observe aquatic life while a mother watched secretly from a window, allowing solitary musings and refraining from praising skills of scientific observation. For a mood of wonder lives under a spell easily broken by the slightest hint of judgment.

We have forgotten what it feels like to be children governed by mysterious principles of growth, by the wondrous experience of Wordsworth's "celestial light" in "the glory and freshness of a dream." As a culture we have lost sight of the fact that it is this childhood glory, this delicate flowering of the inner life of the child that gives rise to the healthy adult.

We need to transform our view of childhood and our roles as parents and teachers. I am not promoting a ten-point program that guarantees success. Instead, as an author, I will use an approach I frequently employ as a teacher. I will tell you a true story. Within the story you will find a spirit that can renew our parenting and teaching, an approach with less manipulation more enchantment, less worry more confidence, less programming more freedom, less testing more singing, less busywork and more real work, more observation less judgment, more conversations and fewer dictates, less anxiety and more wonder.

Dear Reader,

The story is true, but I have, in a few instances, compressed timeframes for a more fluid telling. In spite of an entreaty by certain individuals to use their real names in the book, I have changed the names of my students and most adults.

I do not have the type of memory that captures whole conversations word for word. Yet, sometimes, the class would venture into a territory where the children's words seemed to stop time. While these discussions are reported almost verbatim, I have had to do my best to recreate other conversations.

I begin the telling with deep gratitude to all the children, colleagues, parents, supporters, and visionaries who have made this story possible.

WORKING WITH WONDER

1

Wonder

If a child is to keep alive his inborn sense of wonder, he needs the companionship of at least one adult who can share it, rediscovering with him the joy, excitement and mystery of the world we live in.

—Rachel Carson

WE ARE ABOUT TO ENTER A FIRST GRADE CLASSROOM. It is time for you to let go of thinking and explaining so you can begin a journey to a time before you lived so much in your head. Remember the world of movement, wonder, and intense sensation that you lived in when you were six years old. Take a few minutes to be that six-year-old who is still inside you. Find a memory from your own childhood, a living picture that carries you back to the sense of reality that still hides behind your adult consciousness.

A memory that comes to me is walking in the shade of a tunnel of trees to our mailbox after a summer rain, the warm, damp asphalt under my bare feet, then stepping into a sun-soaked puddle after gazing into the rainbow oil sheen glimmering on the still surface.

I also remember standing on an old, white metal chair under the house-high apple tree, then wrapping my arms around the trunk and pulling myself with all my might into the lower branches to a horseback-shaped seat where I would sit for what seemed like many hours in a home of limbs and leaves filtering dappled sunlight.

If you can, bring that heightened six-year-old sense of full awareness into the present. Find and live in your own childhood memories, then get up and go for a walk and really see and feel the world around you without thoughts of responsibilities, without judgment, without the past or the future. Or toss a ball with your child, or make yourself a cup of hot tea. Remember the form of attention that is rooted in sights, sounds, and smells, in your joy in movement.

Let go of your visions of most schools today, which may include anxiety about testing, days without recess, art, or music, kindergartens without playtime. Instead, be open to a picture of school as it should be, where children and their teachers are eager to step into their classrooms, where each day holds promise.

Then, please join us at nine in the morning in early October of our first grade year, seven first graders and one teacher, in our tiny classroom in a historic captain's house on Cape Cod within smelling distance of the sea. Come in by the front door and tiptoe to the top of the stairs.

You will be coming into our math lesson. We tend to think of the number one as a tiny number: one speck of fluff, one grain of sand, one brick, one cup of flour, small units that when joined together make up milkweed pods, beaches, buildings, and cakes. But, I had hinted at another perspective. The previous day, I had spoken of the number one as a big number, one whole class, one whole school, one whole town. Now it was the children's job to retell the essence of what I had told them, and perhaps to add their own spin to it.

You will enter our classroom as I say "Now, let's remember our story from yesterday." Come in as quietly as you can through the second door on your left and notice six-year-old Helen looking out the window with an expression that says she is far, far away. Watch her tentatively raising her hand, her eyes still unfocused.

You are traveling back in time to 1991. Today, the children in this room are grown. They run businesses, raise children, work as a nurse, a selectman, a horse trainer. In this room, however, they are six years old and about to enter into a conversation both brief and profound.

"Helen," I whispered, not wanting to break her spell. "The number one," she began, "is like the earth and the stars and the sun are all part of one...everything, the whole universe is part of it and it just goes on and on forever."

All eyes grew wide and there was a feeling of searching together.

"It's like when someone dies," Rebecca spoke with a soft certainty. "Someone dies, someone is born. Someone dies, someone is born. It just goes on and on forever." Time seemed to stop as we groped with the infinite, with oneness, with the never-ending continuity of all things.

"Yeah," said Steven, trying to bring this big idea into our everyday reality. He looked at his desk, then looked toward the door. "It's like desks. You take one out, you bring one in, take one out, bring one in." Heads nodded in understanding. Desks were indeed part of the infinite, cosmic order of things.

I had allowed an opening into the cosmic, and then Steven's comment on desks had connected the cosmic with the concrete. An open-eyed sense of wonder still lived in the room, holding us in its spell.

Tanya sensed the change of mood yet still wanted to join this weighty discussion. "Look," she said, pulling a folded cloth napkin out of her desk and putting it on her chest, "I have a little bib." We had been in the clouds, and farther, in the deep reaches of space, where we had touched together the essence of time. But, now we were back on earth in the white schoolhouse where we had work to do, and then snack, complete with a little bib.

But, part of me did not come back. It stayed out there in the far reaches of the galaxy. That evening, and in the weeks ahead, I journeyed to where my first graders had taken me. They had led me to a place I dimly remembered, to the territory of early childhood, to a consciousness in which everything is part of a seamless whole.

At six and seven years old, my children understood truths that they would soon begin to forget. Now it was my job to protect their wonder, knowing that, before long, their dreamy sense of oneness would begin to slip away. Over the next few years, my students would go through a profound transformation. Slowly, in stages, they would fall away from a selfless affinity with all things.

To first graders, every object, every living being has a place in a world strung together by imagination. But, soon, an acorn top would cease to be an elf's cap. A little stone would no longer be a fairy's smooth, rounded seat. It would become a hard, lifeless rock. And the stars of the night sky would no longer dance with the fireflies, but would turn out to be cold, distant specks. Ultimately, by third grade, my students would each perceive themselves to be in a world of discrete objects, and they would see themselves standing apart from a universe that was no longer a never-ending, benign continuity.

Holding a steady course toward wonder would then mean that I needed to become a different kind of teacher. It would be my job to help my students forge new connections with the universe one acorn, one stone, one star at a time. Then I would explain how the amazing phenomenon of photosynthesis leads to the production of acorns. I would describe the volcanic fire and flows of lava that gave birth to the igneous rock. I would bring my students close to the nuclear reactions in the far off stars and tell them that the atoms in their own bones were formed in an ancient stellar blaze. It would be a new sort of reality-based awe that I would need to learn how to kindle when my class ceased to make their own easy connections and understandings.

I had been told in teacher training that in the first two grades, as the children arose from a dreamy ability to create a view of seamless reality, it was my responsibility to guard my class from an awakening that was too startling, too early. The idea was that it was more important to nurture the inner forces behind a child's imagination than to fill that child with too many facts too soon. I had been told that my job was all about patience, setting an unhurried pace.

But now I understood that we are meant to be more than guardians. I realized that, in rare moments, we can behold deep truths freely flowing from the divine consciousness of young children. Allowing them the time to feel and express their wonder also creates an opportunity for children to give adults a priceless gift.

And I saw that, in those moments of cosmic connection, I was meant to be the student of my students and that my devotion to them would lead to my inexpressible reverence for them. It was an uncommon privilege to be among these six- and seven-year-old children who saw what I could not see, who felt what I could not feel on my own. It was remarkable that we had shared a conversation about the continuity of all things. For, an innocent awareness of this continuity belongs to almost all children younger than seven. But, the ability to discuss such matters usually comes later, after this consciousness has dissipated. Ours had been an interlude in which such a nascent understanding and the ability to express it came together for a few transcendent moments.

I had to admit that I, like most adults, was trapped in my head, in a world of concrete information and a connection to time that is measured by responsibilities. We strive for deep inner connections and, whether we know it or not, our seeking is borne of a yearning for what we have lost, the effortless and selfless immersion that is the province of monks and meditators, of holy people and of young children.

While I could no longer live in this holy province, I could try to become more open to it, could be attentive for signs of an opening to the sacred. Then, in precious and unexpected moments I might be invited in. And, in those moments, and in the memory of such moments, I too could dwell in the limitless.

At forty years of age, enchanted by the start up school where my daughter was now in fifth grade, and where I had served as a volunteer and administrator, I had gone back to college to complete a graduate program with a certificate in Waldorf education.

My classroom at the top of the stairs was in a converted bedroom in a historic house that parents and teachers had transformed into a schoolhouse. During August I had washed the classroom floor and arranged the wooden desks and chairs. I had, with help from colleagues and parents, painted our window trim. I had learned songs, poems, and dances and prepared a story to tell from memory. I had visited each of my first graders at their homes where I had admired Rebecca's new red shoes, enjoyed Nellie's precocious conversational skills and had been astounded by Jamie's wild antics. The night before that first auspicious morning, I drew a colorful picture on the blackboard and placed a crystal vase of cool water on my small, oak desk.

In the ecology of childhood, the first grade year, the meeting place of the era of early childhood and the grade school years, is like the salt marsh, that protected space where the land meets the sea. Both first grade and the salt marsh are places where two worlds meet, and a richness arises that neither realm possesses alone. The salt marsh is among the richest zones of biodiversity on earth and the turning point that comes at seven years old is, perhaps, the human equivalent, a node of promise and potential in the human journey.

On that first day of school, teachers, forty-one grade school students, and their parents had gathered on the new mown grass for our opening assembly. Behind the teachers, two enormous maple trees shaded the front patio of the small kindergarten building. These trees framed a low, white picket fence. At the center of that fence a gate opened to a white manse that was once a sea captain's house, now our grade school building.

My class of seven had stood before me. This was the first day that they would walk through the picket gate and enter the big white building as grade school students. On this cool September morning, these six-year-old children would emerge from the warm cocoon of their kindergarten years and ascend, with me, to the second floor.

I had noticed Rebecca's scarlet shoes and returned Nellie's confident smile. I worried that Jamie would repeat the wild antics I had seen during my visit to his home.

Fifth graders, the oldest children in the school that year, presented a long-stemmed pink rose to each of my little students. I told a special story. Then, with everyone watching, I led my awed little ones away from the crowd, across the lawn and through the picket gate. We had been the first to enter the big white house. We climbed up the stairs to our classroom, a room that still looked a bit like a small bedroom. Each child slid a rose into the vase. They spotted their names on their desks and everyone, even Jamie, sat down politely. They looked up at me with an air of wondrous expectation that matched my own.

We had become like a family, my seven children and I, five girls and two boys. I could fit the whole class into my van and drive ten miles down the bay to visit the school's satellite kindergarten. We could walk to the pond, the baseball field or to the harbor on a whim. I could sit for many minutes by a child who needed help and not worry that someone else was being ignored.

But there were times when we wished the class were bigger, when we wanted to sing loudly, have enough players for kickball, or enough actors for our play.

"It's not fair," said Jamie, "if Steven is absent, I don't have a boy to play with. "Yeah," said Steven, "same for me if Jamie is absent."

One Sunday in late October, I hauled buckets of soil, trays of moss, and an old drawer from a discarded bureau up to the classroom. I filled the drawer with the soil and molded it into hills and valleys. Then I laid a quilt of dark green moss, light green moss, short dense moss and loose, thick moss across the hills and dales so that the square in front of the bright south facing window looked like the green countryside as viewed from an airplane far above. Into this moss garden I placed little trees and rocks and, in the deepest hollow, a clamshell full of water.

The children gathered around the new fairyland on Monday morning, stroking the soft moss as they would stroke a kitten. "If I was a fairy I would sit on this rock and put my feet in the water," said Tanya.

I encouraged the children to contribute nature treasures to our moss garden, so soon the hills and valleys became adorned with pinecones, acorns, rose hips, jingle shells, and a long stem of milkweed pods. I moved the milkweed stem to a window ledge above the garden where it would dry in the sun.

One day during class, as the sun streamed across the mossy hills, one of the milkweed pods popped open and ejected a fluffy parasol bearing a seed. Sally pointed to it and we all gazed in wonder as the downy parachute floated across the classroom. It was followed by a second parasol and a third.

"You know," I said, "each of these parasols could be a wish for a new child to come to our class next year." Nellie's eyes still tracked the parasol. "So, maybe we'll have three new friends."

"I hope they're boys," said Jamie, "then we'll be even."

"Nice mathematical thinking," I mused, smiling at Jamie. He wasn't looking at me. I followed his astounded gaze back to the high window ledge. The pod had burst wide open into a cumulous, pulsating mass. The slight breeze from the other window tickled the fluff, coaxing bits of down into the air. Suddenly the room was clouded with milkweed down.

Then something happened, something that would happen again and again over my six years with my class, something of gigantic importance, yet imperceptible. It had happened when we spoke about the oneness of the universe and the limitless continuity of all things. It was a simple, silent shift in the manner of the class prompted by a decision on my part to step back and allow the children to lead the way. I made no pronouncement. My turning the reins over to the class was a silent passing of leadership.

The transformation was like the sudden flight of the milkweed parasols. One moment we were snug in the pod of our classroom, sitting in chairs at little desks, bound together by rules, by habits, by order and routine, and then, suddenly, and silently, after a nod from me, the children rose from their chairs. I smiled as the children appeared to float up in sync with the moving milkweed, as they stepped up onto their seats, some blowing gently at the white fluff, others holding out their hands as landing pads. For a minute that felt like an eternity, we moved wordlessly in slow motion awe, as if our energized silence would keep the downy fluff aloft.

There are some who think that each moment of every school day should be bound by rules and procedures and there are others who maintain that total freedom is best for the developing child. Myself, I prefer the dance we discovered that day and in all days to come, an improvised choreography of order and spontaneity.

Then our levity made us giggle. Nellie laughed, "I guess we'll have hundreds of new classmates next year."

"Boys *and* girls," said Tanya looking pointedly at Jamie.

The children took the intact pods out to recess where they popped them open and chased the parasols on the wind. And, already thinking about writing my teaching story, I remembered our wish for each milkweed parasol to predict that someone new would join our class and envisioned and welcomed the hundreds of readers who would someday travel through time to our tiny classroom to be part of our journey.

2

Confidence

...in education you must take the whole human being into consideration—the growing, living human being, and not just an abstract idea. It is only when you have the right conception of human life as a connected whole that you come to realize how different from each other the various ages are.

—Rudolf Steiner

SALLY GAZED at fleets of paper-brown oak leaves sailing in the wind outside our window. It was the end of snack and she had eaten slowly and not much. Now, with her big brown eyes drinking in the flotillas of autumn, she seemed to take her nourishment from her vision of fairy skyboats.

If I had not known that Steven was Sally's fraternal twin, I would not have guessed it. They were both small and delicate in appearance, but Sally's hair and eyes were deep brown while Steven's hair was sandy and his eyes were hazel. And, while Sally was shy, Steven was outgoing. While Sally played fantasy games under the bushes at recess, Steven had recently begun playing touch football with the big kids. Now, while Sally's snack still lay half-eaten on her desk, Steven sat behind a closed lunchbox, ready to go out to play.

A rumble of feet filled the hallway and underscored the high tones of second grade voices on their way out to recess. Steven brightened and sat up straighter. Jamie, Rebecca, and Nellie also sat poised to join the older class. Sally looked at her apple.

I opened the door to the hallway and said, "It's cold outside, children. Remember to wear mittens and hats and to zip your jackets."

Steven and his three cohorts darted by me. Sally took a contemplative bite from her apple. Helen and Tanya lingered over multiple open containers of food.

Stepping into the narrow hallway and taking my coat off the hook, I moved to a vantage point where I could see into three separate realms. These were all children moving toward the big transformation that comes at nine years old, all moving through the little changes that would lead to the big change in third grade.

With Steven and three of his classmates now in the hall, the interior of our room had become Sally's world, where Sally, Helen, and Tanya still lived in a timeless kingdom of young children, a realm of dreamy sensations. It was peopled by little folk who speak and eat slowly, who see fairies amid the fluttering leaves. In that world, my three most deliberate first graders slowly and carefully closed plastic food containers and gently placed them in wicker baskets and metal lunchboxes.

Just outside our door, I saw Steven's world, a land of transition, where children live in both sensation and in time, and in the quest to prove themselves. When children find themselves in this new territory, they come to care about feeling competent, and want to prove that they are no longer little kids. Now their experience of what is wondrous includes both fairies and their amazement at their own abilities. In this land, children begin to look ahead, to anticipate recess, lunch, and being in second grade.

First graders cross an invisible threshold into this transitional realm on their own schedule. This development has nothing to do with their intelligence, but is more like the mystery of losing one's baby teeth and growing big teeth. Progress toward this transition cannot be rushed nor can it be slowed down. And, even twins enter into this time of transformation according to their personal internal clocks.

This was no ordinary moment. It was, in fact, just what I as a new teacher was waiting for, a moment when I could see on my own both the essence of the developmental stages in my class and something of the character of each child in it.

Rudolf Steiner, the founder of Waldorf education, hoped teachers would cultivate ever-deeper perceptions of each child. It would be years before I was able to meet a child for the first time and, simply by observing them, say, "You are seven years old," or "You are almost ten." Now in the hallway as I surveyed the three groups, I was just beginning to take in images of body language, expression, and ways of moving that over many years would bring me to an intuitive understanding of what it means to be seven, eight, or nine.

According to Rudolf Steiner, and the ninety years of practice by teachers cultivating such intuitions, this ability to perceive the needs of both the individual and the age was a key to effective teaching. How else could one know what or how to teach if one did not know what the child was able to comprehend or able to do? How else could one choose material that a child would consider wonderful if one was not tuned in to what children at each developmental step hungered for?

Just outside the visible threshold of our classroom, Jamie, Rebecca, and Nellie, acutely aware that they were holding up the bigger kids, quickly fastened their jackets. Steven's face tightened into a grimace as he tried again and again to start his zipper.

Farther down the narrow corridor stood an agitated, but now silent, line of children who lived in a third realm, that of second graders. These students lived squarely in the region of time and intention. And their intention was to get out to recess. They looked back and forth between me and Steven who still fumbled with his coat.

I took Steven by the hand, smiled at the long row of children and gestured for them to pass us. While I crouched to Steven's level to zip his coat, the well-bundled mob thundered down the stairs. As their last reverberations dissipated, my three remaining girls emerged from the classroom and quietly claimed the peaceful hallway for the territory of early childhood.

I noticed that the other upstairs teacher, who did not have recess duty, had her eye on the hallway.

"See you outside after you dress warmly," I said to three girls as they dreamily looked out the hall window, still holding their lunches. Steven was already out of sight.

When I emerged from the building, the fourth grade teacher already stood at the sidelines of a game of touch football. I joined him watching fourth and fifth grade boys and girls, trailed by younger children, charging up and down the small field. Steven and Jamie, with no sense of strategy and no hope that a big kid would ever direct the football to them, ran hither and yon, always toward the ball, never touching it.

Steven did not look frustrated, or tired. At each turn, he reached a new level of determination. He set his eye on the ball and accelerated to top speed. When the ball was caught, or there was a change in trajectory, he stopped, turned, and initiated a new furious, but futile, charge.

"Your kids sure are small," my colleague said, shaking his head.

"I guess first graders always seem small," I replied, laughing.

"I mean even smaller than most first graders. If I didn't know how old they were I would guess most of them were in preschool."

He was right. Rebecca and Sally were not only tiny, but they still had the rounder cheeks of little kids. But tiny in body doesn't mean tiny in spirit. Steven was the smallest kid out there, but he was more determined than anyone else on the field. And, in spite of never getting close to the ball, he loved playing with the big kids more than anything. Here, on the field, he was finding a route to self-confidence that relied on his own accomplishments. As I watched Steven zoom around the field, I remembered my own childhood accomplishment of climbing the apple tree in our front yard.

Parents and teachers today often speak about children being proud of their accomplishments, but pride is not what I remember as I reached the top of that 20-foot-tall tree and poked my head out the top. What I remember feeling was amazement. I was amazed at what I saw, and I was amazed that I had scaled this tree on my own. My sense was that Steven was also awed by his abilities. Even if he was not getting a chance to carry the ball, he was, to a large extent, keeping up with the big kids and this was new to him. When we experience a new capacity, our first feeling is wonder.

I saw Nellie running toward me around the edge of the field. "Tanya says I can't come into her house," she panted.

"OK, I'll come," I said.

I skirted the field with Nellie and crawled with her into Tanya's "house," a cosy den under a drooping bush. I huddled with the two girls and helped them find a peaceful understanding. Emerging from my peacemaking visit, I was just in time to see Steven about to collide with Kyle, one of the biggest fifth graders. Many voices, including my own, shouted a jumble of warnings: "Kyle, watch out!"

"Steven!"

"Kyle, stop!"

Alerted too late, Kyle tried to stop, but Steven kept running. It was not the full speed crash it might have been, but Kyle was thrown off balance by the impact and his last second braking. He crumbled on top of Steven and the two boys fell together. Unhurt, Kyle jumped up quickly and leaned over Steven, who winced and clutched his leg. The fourth grade teacher and I converged on the accident from opposite sides of the field.

"Steven, are you OK?" I asked, kneeling and bending over him.

He stood up, brushed off his pants and faced me eye to eye. "I'm fine," he said.

I reached out to draw him closer, thinking he could use a hug, but he stepped back, smiled, turned and ran toward the other kids, ready to play ball.

"Lucky," said my colleague. "He's a resilient little guy, but I think we can't count on his luck holding."

This was the first year we had fifth graders in the school, so it was the first year we had fifth graders playing fast running games with first graders. As we shepherded children toward the building at the end of recess we discussed the risks involved in allowing six-year-old and eleven-year-old children to play touch football together and we agreed to bring the issue to faculty meeting on Tuesday after school. I decided that the next day I would take the class for a walk to the community playground at recess time. That way we could keep the first graders out of the game until after the meeting.

Nora, my fifth grade daughter, her friend Brian, and I walked toward home after school. This journey was usually a pleasant half hour stroll when I reviewed the school day and looked toward the morrow. But, today, with Steven's crash on my mind, the pleasant stroll had become an agitated march.

I tramped through heaps of leaves while imagining the upcoming faculty meeting. It was obvious that we would acknowledge that fifth graders and first graders, especially extra small first graders, should not play touch football together.

I foresaw a quick discussion that would result in a new recess rule. And this rule, I feared, would be a blow to Steven's spirit that he would feel longer and more deeply than his collision with Kyle. He had experienced the wonder of his own speed in a game with older children, and it was my job to provide opportunities for wonder, not to take them away. Yet, I had to keep him safe and a collision with an eighty-pound fifth grader could put Steven in the hospital. I could already hear myself saying, "The teachers have decided that it is too dangerous for first graders to play touch football with the older kids."

I could already see Steven's disappointed face. I could see him losing his eagerness for recess. I was concerned that losing the sense of awe at his newfound abilities could make Steven feel that he was no longer capable. In fact, I could see him losing much of the self-assurance I had worked so hard to nurture in these early months of first grade. I knew that losing the perk of playing football with the big kids would not be enough to irreparably harm Steven's spirit. Yet, I was wary. A series of such blows to self-confidence can have a cumulative effect.

The process of working with wonder is not simple. For most people—children as well as adults—a sense of health, safety, belongingness and self-esteem constitute the hull, keel, rigging, and sails that allow us to catch the wind of wonder. A big part of the job of teachers and parents who are committed to working with wonder is attending to the maintenance of all aspects of the metaphoric ships in their care.

Children emerging from the wonderland of early childhood, who are on the threshold of the competence-seeking realm of grade school children, often need extra care. We wish to draw forth each child's natural sense of amazement when first discovering his or her own capabilities and slowly build a stable confidence that comes with growing mastery. Most schools reward such competence through praise, test scores, and grades. But, teachers who work with wonder know that these external messages tend to pull students' attention from their own sense of awe about a new ability to a growing awareness of and dependence upon the teacher's evaluations. If we are not careful, too much emphasis on praise and grades, on compliments and declarations of pride, can cause a newly rooted sense of self-confidence to be pushed aside by feelings of anxiety about pleasing adults. This is why teachers and parents who work with wonder in the early grade school years must take care to refrain from expressing too much judgment and instead need to find ways to help the child experience and value his or her growing abilities.

I wanted my kids to forget that they were the littlest kids in the grade school. I wanted them to feel ageless and wise, for that is how I saw them. I especially wanted Steven to feel that his inner being, the source of the feisty determination that drove him to face off with giants on the football field, was his true self.

Now it was Monday afternoon. On Wednesday morning, Steven would be handed a different perception when his age and diminutive size would be put before him as his defining features. He was at a precarious point: his sense of wonder was in transition from being centered in a world of imagination to a new center that had to do with amazement about the real world and his own capacities. The last message I wanted coming to Steven during this transition was anything that implied he was not a highly capable human being. While it was far from my inclination to reward competence, it was my job to support Steven's natural, uncomplicated belief in and amazement about his own abilities.

But this unfortunate wake up call was coming as surely as the dawn.

My frustration moved into my feet. Leaning into the cold sea wind, I took longer, faster strides. Nora and Brian bounded ahead as we passed the colony of boarded up summerhouses and began the gentle downslope toward the water. By the time they reached the last stretch before the harbor, they were far ahead of me.

The two children skirted the foot of a steep hill covered by looming pine trees. There was something about this scene in which the two children appeared so small and the forest so huge that reminded me of an image from a Grimm's fairy tale. It was an image that brought to mind something I could give to Steven, to Jamie, to the whole class, something that might help them hold on to deeper, truer perceptions of themselves.

Back at the silent school building after dinner, I drew quickly until the chalk picture covered half the blackboard. I usually put my board drawings on the small blackboard at the side of the room, but I put this one on the big front board, where it would be in the children's field of view for much of the day. I added bits of yellow to highlight the dark green leaves of the newly felled tree that filled most of the drawing. Then, I dipped my dusty, chalk-covered hands in a bucket of water and dried them before I stood back to consider where to place the lead character in the stories I planned to tell on Tuesday and Wednesday. Finally, I stepped back to the board and sketched a figure sitting in the tree. He was jaunty, well dressed, and far smaller than the children in my class. He was, in fact, no larger than a leaf. He was one of my favorite characters from Grimm's Fairy Tales, Tom Thumb.

The next morning Nellie was first to spot him, "Hey look!" she said. "There's a little man hiding in that tree."

"Yeah" said Steven. "He sure is small."

"Even smaller than a leaf," I said.

"Is he going to be in our story today, Mrs. Allsup?" asked Jamie.

"We'll see." I said, smiling and raising my eyebrows. One way to keep wonder alive is to keep children wondering.

Tom Thumb was indeed in our story that morning. When I told

the part about the woman giving birth to a baby no larger than a thumb, everyone smiled and pointed at the little figure in the tree. Then, they listened in amazement, as they heard about how little Tom led a horse by talking into his ear, tricked a thief by running down a mouse hole, and endured being swallowed by a cow.

Our week transpired as I expected. The class enjoyed the extra playground trips that kept them away from the touch football games. The teachers issued a new rule about keeping first graders out of fast running games with fifth graders. I told the class about the new rule that we had instituted for their safely and Steven said, "It's not fair." Nellie said, "We're going to the playground today anyway." Steven looked down at his feet and repeated in a soft, dull voice, "It's still not fair." Realizing that this was one of those rare instances when praise can be helpful, I spoke briefly about how Steven and Jamie were such good football players. Jamie brightened, but Steven crossed his arms and scowled.

When we reviewed the Tom Thumb story on the day after I announced the new rule, I asked questions about how Tom Thumb faced challenges posed by being so tiny. Nellie, Tanya, and Jamie talked about how little Tom made the best of things and used his small size to advantage. I hoped that Steven would raise his hand and say something that hinted that he, too, had found a soul mate in Tom Thumb, that he was able to move beyond his disappointment about not playing football with the big kids because he knew that the new rule could not take away the incredible essence of his being. But, instead, he looked far away and I wondered if he was paying attention.

Over the next few days, I listened as we worked on writing and drawing projects about this feisty little character. Unfortunately, Steven said nothing about Tom Thumb and nothing more about the recess rule. I watched Steven for signs that he felt frustrated or sad.

Sometimes, I convinced myself that he had indeed taken a step onto the pathway of disaffection, that he seemed quieter and more introspective. But, then I would see him flying off the jungle gym wearing a huge grin.

The following week brought a day when I had other responsibilities at recess, when I could not bring the class to the playground, when Steven would not only be banned from the football game but would find himself watching it from the sidelines.

"You are going to recess with the second grade today, class." I said as we moved into the transition between snack and recess. Everyone packed up their lunch boxes quickly and moved out the door, even Sally, Helen, and Tanya, everyone except for Steven.

The cacophony of voices in the hall was quelled by an announcement by the second grade teacher.

Steven gazed beyond where I sat at my desk as he silently picked up his lunchbox and came to stand by me. Then, I realized that he was not looking idly into space as I'd thought, but was riveted to the picture of Tom Thumb sitting in a tree that still covered half the chalkboard.

He would, in a few moments, let me zip his jacket. Then he would head out to recess where he and Jamie would invent a modified game of touch football for two people in which they each actually got to handle the ball.

But, as he stood by my desk, while the rumble of feet moved down the stairs and out of the building, I didn't know that yet. I still wondered about his inner journey in the days since the announcement of the new rule. I wondered too whether he was oblivious to the role model I had put before him, of a little man, so much like himself, whose indomitable spirit made his physical size unimportant.

Finally, when the white school building felt as empty and silent as a sun-bleached beach shell, Steven spoke. He didn't offer a dissertation on how his new relationship with Tom Thumb helped him deal with his disappointment. He said only a few words, but, for me, they were enough to let me know that he was going to be okay.

"Mrs. Allsup," he said, gazing adoringly at the jaunty little person in the tree, "I love that picture."

3

Curiosity

The need for imagination, a sense of truth, a feeling of responsibility, these are the three forces which are the very nerves of pedagogy. And whoever will receive pedagogy into himself, let him inscribe the following as a motto for his teaching:

Imbue thyself with the power of imagination
Have courage for the truth
Sharpen thy feeling for responsibility of soul.

—Rudolf Steiner

MARCH ON CAPE COD, a peninsula enveloped by the frigid winter Atlantic, is a cold month. The transition to springtime in the third week is a mere technicality. On Monday of that early March week, it was snowing by the time we left school. The snow fell into the night, then ended, so, by morning, the streets were plowed, and a thick, white blanket lay on the playground.

I had been teaching for six months, and, like a person discovering a penchant for sighting rare shore birds, I had developed a new quest. You never know when the elusive piping plover will emerge from its well-camouflaged nesting area and dance down the shoreline. You just have to go to the beach, and watch and wait and hope. And you can't plan for the sublime moments when the children themselves look out into the universe or deep into their own souls and grasp something that only they can reach for, that you could not hand them ready made.

I lived for those moments, waited for them, watching for the far off gaze, the first tentative words that would begin a journey that I could support but could not lead. We called the first two hours of each day "main lessons." But these sublime moments often taught me my main lessons.

Recently, I had begun to greet Tuesdays with mixed emotions. The best part was knitting class. Unlike main lesson, when I initiated the conversation, the topics raised in knitting class arose from the children themselves. This forty-minute period, while we sat in a circle with yarn and needles, was like a trip to the beach at dawn, when the birds owned the littoral zone before the arrival of the sunbathers, a time when one might hope to be graced by the unexpected.

Now, with the spring enrollment campaign underway, knitting was preceded, however, by something I dreaded, the parent tour and talk. The tour was conducted by our administrator, but the talk was my job. It was for parents considering the school and I thought I was expected to speak like some sort of expert, not like myself, a novice teacher, feeling my way cautiously through each day.

I met the group of four visitors in the activity room that adjoined our classroom. I knew they were all considering a big step. Would they forgo free neighborhood schools to commit thousands of dollars in tuition over eight years to an unproven institution, only seven years old?

Somehow, in less than twenty minutes, I was supposed to show why our parents, who generally had average incomes, were willing to make not only the financial sacrifice, but also to provide daily chauffeur service, serve on committees, paint classrooms and take a turn every couple of months as the school's weekend janitor.

I began by telling them an experience I had every year when my son was in public school. Each spring a new teacher would tell me, "Ben is so quiet, I am just getting to know him." Then, in June, he would be sent on to a new teacher where, again, he would be an unknown child.

As I spoke about how the long-term relationship with the class teacher allows us to maintain a deep connection with every child, I considered what to say next. I had twenty minutes to distill what I had learned about this unique form of education in eight years as a Waldorf parent, a year of Waldorf foundation courses, a year of teacher training and six months of teaching. I knew I could not say it all, so I took advice from Rudolf Steiner who suggested ways to deliver complex topics to students. Focus, he said, on what he called symptomatology; give a few good examples, and tell stories that make the lessons come alive.

"Of course," I continued, "I knew, as I am sure that you do, that children go through developmental phases. I remember my mother saying when I was a young teen, 'Oh she's just going through a stage.'" Sometimes we think of these phases in our children's lives as an annoying set of characteristics that we have to put up with until the next stage presents a new set of challenges.

"When we go a bit deeper, though, and read the theories of the classic child development experts like Piaget and Gessell, we find that there is something fascinating about the way every child moves through a new consciousness and a new set of abilities each year." I shared my memories about my son in sixth grade, his growing ability to solve problems, to think analytically, to hold his own in an argument, was part of the special territory of every sixth grader. So was his sense that he should be able to make his own decisions.

"Rudolf Steiner's stroke of genius," I told the politely listening parents folded into first grade chairs, "was related to these stages of consciousness. Like Piaget and Gessell, he recognized the importance of the predictable inner evolution experienced by each child. But then he took a brilliant step. He realized that the questions, the worries, the proclivities, and the abilities of each age provide openings toward certain themes. He predicted that children would experience a deep sense of satisfaction by being given the right topics at the right time. Of course, all school curricula are built on the idea that children are more capable each year. But this was more than that. To Steiner, the child's growing abilities were important, but equally important was the new worldview that came with each age and grade.

"The analytical sixth grader, for instance, is newly able to handle concepts and processes that are more abstract than those he or she could comprehend in fourth or fifth grade. But this is more than a new ability. Steiner saw that students at this age have a strong desire to think logically, to see and to make their own order in the world. The consciousness of a sixth grader, he said, is like the consciousness of people in ancient Rome. So, at this age we learn about Roman statesmen engaged in long, logical arguments, and how their ambition to order the world led to the great Roman Empire. The sixth grader who has an urge to negotiate a sharing of power with his or her parents will be intrigued by many aspects of Roman history including the way the Romans allowed territories they conquered to continue to manage their own internal affairs. The children, of course do not know that we have chosen Roman History in grade six or a Norse Mythology in grade four because they are likely to be fascinated by these topics because that relate to their own inner changes."

"This is a very small example of how the Waldorf curriculum is designed to matter deeply to children. The content of all the subjects studied each year is truly soul food for the students."

I briefly reviewed the curriculum through the early grades and described how the themes relate to each developmental phase. I talked about how physical movement and art is integrated into everything we do. I explained how lessons in knitting, beeswax modeling, and woodwork develop both dexterous hands and nimble minds and how all of this develops confidence and engagement. I began to take questions. Then, there was a knock at the door. It was the teacher who was leaving my class and now had to move along to a different group of children. I stood up, surprised at how quickly the time had gone, and began to say a rather ungracious goodbye.

"Relax," she said, "sit down and take a few more minutes. I told the class it sounded like you were still busy with our visitors. They had the idea they would set up the room without you. Don't tell them I told you, they want it to be a surprise."

I heard muffled voices and the scraping of desks and chairs in the next room as I ended my conversation with the visiting parents. Moments later when I stepped into the first grade classroom, my seven angels were sitting in a circle, already knitting. I saw that they had followed our usual furniture-moving routine. The desks now lined the wall and seven little chairs and my teacher's chair formed a circle all facing a wicker basket in the middle, piled high with colored yarn.

"You set up this room so well, you remind me of second graders," I said as I sat down and took Tanya's knitting and considered what to do about a gaping hole.

I noticed that Sally and Rebecca were knitting steadily and that Jamie and Steven were waiting for me to unravel whatever predicament they had knitted themselves into. I ripped out Tanya's last two rows, and knitted one replacement row for her and reached out for Steven's knitting when Jamie opened a conversation.

"Everything is made out of atoms," declared Jamie.

I smiled and asked, "Where did you learn about atoms?"

"From my Dad," said Jamie brightly.

"What are atoms?" Rebecca asked. She was wearing a pink sweatshirt decorated with puffy fabric paint. The theme was teddy bears and puffy white dots.

"Atoms are just like those dots on your sweatshirt, only smaller," explained Jamie.

Tanya shook her head vigorously and said, "Oh no. I am not made of those little white dots."

Facing this disbelief, Jamie sought a little back up. "Mrs. Allsup, isn't it true? Aren't we made of atoms? Isn't everything made of atoms?"

It would have been possible to give an elementary lecture on physics, but my sense was that holding back on explanations would create an opening for exploration, for their attempts, perhaps, to envision on their own the notion that the world is composed of tiny dots. It was this ability to imagine how things worked, to delve into the questions on their own, that was going to eventually help them to develop an inner picture of the nature of matter. Learning how to live with questions, how to try on answers, toss them aside, and try again, that was the essence of learning at any age. Here they were, first graders, doing just that, asking questions about, of all things, the essence of matter.

So, I left the door open and asked, "What do you all think?"

Rebecca challenged, "Well, if we are made of atoms, what makes them all stick together?"

Jamie's quick reply may not have been technically correct, but, more important, it showed good thinking: "What do you think your skin is for?"

We finished knitting and ate lunch. Another teacher had recess duty, and I had a meeting with our school's advisor, Torin Finser. Not long ago, Torin had been one of my teachers at Antioch New England Graduate School where he ran the Waldorf program. I looked forward to his visits to our fledgling school, but I was nervous about his evaluation of my teaching based on his recent visit to a main lesson.

Our tiny classroom grew even smaller as Torin stepped in. He glanced at the top of the doorway and saw that he was going to just make it without ducking. What would it be like, I wondered, to go through life aware of the height restrictions imposed by low doorways? Offering him my grown-up chair, I crunched behind a first grade desk and took a deep breath.

Sitting in a tiny chair, looking up at a looming figure while waiting for a long list of my failings, I felt like one of my first graders on a hard day—one of those days when the zipper won't catch, the knitting becomes a knot, when the wrong word is copied from the board and the whole page is messed up and there is nobody to play with at recess.

I welcomed the list of minor suggestions that might improve my teaching, but I dreaded Torin's ultimate judgment. I was trying to teach my class in a way that made them more devoted to curiosity than concern about my judgments, yet I had not yet entered the consciousness I wished for my students. Like many adults in our culture, I was enslaved by my own perpetual concerns about the judgments of others.

I remembered my evaluation meeting at the end of my student teaching when my supervisor had shared her thoughts about different aspects of my lesson and finished with the observation that I was, "too much in my head," and had recommended that I postpone teaching young children until I had more experience with older children.

Now I saw that she had been perceptive. My children were teaching me that appeals based on logic did not work. I was learning not to say, "We can get out to recess sooner if we can settle down and concentrate on our writing." Instead, I found that a little song or a tune on my recorder brought a cheerful note into the room and led my children through a transition into work in a way that was more pleasant than a logical explanation.

I had learned too that only instinct, not a well thought out plan, would tell me the moment when I should stop working on my math or spelling lesson and allow the children to lead the way into something more profound than I could teach them. I had learned that the struggle to retain a child's self-confidence matters as much or more than my efforts to fill his head with facts. And I had glimpsed the power of a child's deep inner connection with a lesson to make learning easy, meaningful, and fun.

Now, six months into my first year of teaching, I was beginning my journey to the heart of teaching. I was learning so much everyday about the consciousness of the young child, striving to find my way to their worldview. My intuitive sense of how far I had to go made me feel especially vulnerable as I waited for Torin's judgment.

It didn't help that he did not just get it over with and give me the list of my failings. Instead, we talked about the school's upcoming move from the cramped, old house to a rented public school building and we discussed the school's financial health.

"I suppose this class is not carrying its financial weight," I said. "With only seven students, the tuitions barely pay my salary and the class doesn't contribute to the rent or to the salaries of all the other teachers who work with the class."

"Actually," said Torin, "That's what I'd like to talk about. I've been thinking about your small class and about the upcoming first grade of about twelve children. I think you could teach them all together in a combined class of nineteen students. The big building the school is moving to next year will even have a classroom that will hold nineteen students," he laughed, looking at our room that was a converted bedroom, a converted, small bedroom. "And, it would be a healthier class size financially and for the social life of the students."

He smiled at me in a way that inspired confidence, "I think you could do it."

I gulped. I remembered the hundreds of fluffy milkweed parachutes that had floated across our classroom. Nineteen was not hundreds, but at that moment, I felt that it might as well be.

"I'll think about it." I said.

"Good," he said. "Take your time, it's a big decision."

He discussed the lesson he observed in a general way, but left without ever giving me a list of my shortcomings as a teacher.

I was left to wonder whether he simply forgot to offer a critique of the lesson he had observed or whether he looked at me, a new first grade teacher, the way I looked at my new first grade students. Perhaps he realized that I, too, was beginning a difficult journey and that, like my students, a key to success was not to dwell on my faults, but to help me see my strengths. He had offered me an image of my ability to handle a combined class the same way I had offered Steven the story of the indomitable Tom Thumb. And, like Steven, I had to cogitate for a while to figure out whether I, too, loved the picture that had been put before me.

The next day my class and the second grade built snow forts, a girls' fort and a boys' fort. As I watched the two grade levels working together I realized that, if I accepted the combined class, my classroom would include the full range of ages I now saw hauling loads of snow.

This group of nineteen children with a two year age span cooperated well for fort building. But, would it be possible to meet the needs of each child in such a diverse group in a classroom environment? I thought of the curriculum that I had described to our visitors. With such a mix of ages, how could I be true to one of the main tenets of our educational method, that the lesson content is meant to connect deeply with the child's developmental stage?

I remembered the conversation about atoms as I watched two different strategies for fort building. The boys carried armloads of snow and dumped it in a big clump. The girls formed snowballs about one foot in diameter and piled them up. After awhile, the boys noticed that the girls' fort was growing more quickly than their own. They quit the clump method and began working with atoms.

I thought about Rebecca's question: what holds it all together? Was this a question that arose from a six-year-old's awareness of the interconnectedness of all things? Wasn't this a question that atomic physicists asked? Do little children living in a realm of innocent wonder know all the important questions? If we listened carefully to them, would we rediscover deep questions we have forgotten?

And I grappled with my own questions. I practiced what I wanted my kids to learn to do: I tried on answers, tossed them aside and tried again.

Would I accept responsibility for a combined class? Was I still too intellectual, too much in my head, to do a good job with young children? Would I have to function as the force that bound these two age levels into one coherent group, would I have to be the skin that held it all together? Or, would the children mold themselves into one integrated class? Were my class and the current kindergartners meant to be a single class? Would mysterious forces, akin to subatomic forces, or the forces that draw us into a seamless universe, bind them into a cohesive group? Is wonder one of those forces, or is it a condition that will be beyond our reach if I am trying to meet the needs of multiple developmental groups?

I put my questions aside. I would live with them a bit longer before making my decision. I watched the children molding damp snow into big round balls, and watched them stack the balls higher and higher into walls that grew into massive white barricades that stood tall and strong without nails or mortar or even skin.

4

Attention

My Head bears the being of the resting Stars.
My Breast harbors the life of the wandering Stars.
My Body lives and moves amid the Elements.
This am I.

—Rudolf Steiner

MY FIRST AND SECOND graders streamed past me in the hallway as the recess teacher called my attention to a lone figure on the playground, "Reesa is still wandering around. She never did line up when I called the class."

I looked down the wide hall at my busy flock opening lockers and tugging at jackets outside our spacious classroom. Then I looked out at the bright playground where my lost sheep wandered. Situations like this would lead to new procedure in which the recess teachers held the whole group outside until all were lined up. But, at this moment, our school was still establishing methods and habits. I found myself supervising a group in the hallway and a lone child visible through the big windows in the heavy green doors on the north side of the big brick school building we were now renting from the town.

Reesa was lost in golden October. Shining maple trees bridged the concrete walk down the gentle hill. Brown-gold fallen leaves carpeted the hillside. Bright gold leaves floated toward this mottled carpet where, upon landing, they glittered like brilliant stars.

Alone in this golden splendor, Reesa seemed unaware that she should be with her classmates. Tall, slender, and light on her feet, she

33

danced gleefully from falling leaf to falling leaf, catching a dazzling yellow bouquet of falling stars. While many of her classmates had entered the big girl and big boy world of first graders who want to accomplish tasks and to please adults, Reesa was one of my new first graders who could still be lost in wonder, who danced in the innocent fairyland of early childhood.

Inside, the children began to file into the classroom. This was one of those moments that teachers try to avoid—when one cannot see the entire class at once. In my mind's eye, however, I could see my more mature children settling down at their desks. I knew that they had let go of their game the instant they were called in from recess, that some had trudged, and some had run, directly up the hill. And, I knew that, at this moment, they were looking at the front of the room where I should be standing.

I had agreed, with some trepidation, to taking the combined class. Even with a small class of seven I had often found myself in situations in which I had to choose between serving one student and serving the whole group. And, I had learned that, even when I was teaching only one grade level, I would sometimes be called upon to meet the needs of two different developmental stages.

This year it was worse. The bigger, multi-aged group included at least three developmental groups and created a never-ending stream of challenging situations. I often wondered whether I had taken on a challenge too great for my limited abilities as a rookie teacher. Now, another such situation called for me to be in two places at the same moment.

I was tempted to open the door and call out to Reesa. I knew I had only seconds before I must return to the room or risk disruption. But I didn't call out. I wanted Reesa to learn to line up with the class. But I also wanted her to have this sacred moment. I made one of the one thousand judgment calls a teacher in a wonder-centered school makes each day. I just waited.

Still clutching a handful of leaves, the golden treasure that had lured her into lateness, Reesa skipped and twirled her way up the hill, her light-brown hair flying. As she approached the steps, I stood back from the door where she could not see me and attempted to phrase a gentle reprimand. The door opened, and, as she entered the silent hallway, confusion clouded her pixie-like face. I realized as she turned toward me that it was only at that moment that she became aware that I had been watching her, aware that her classmates were already at their desks, aware that she was late.

Reesa looked at her bouquet. She looked up at me and back to her leaves. Then, gazing into my eyes with sincere remorse, she thrust the shining stars into my hands and transformed the cause of her tardiness into a gift that accompanied her apology. "Here," she said sweetly, "this is because I'm late."

Life is a dance between work and play, between responsibility and pleasure, between listening to the line-up call and being lost in the wonder of twirling, golden leaves. Sometimes, in moments of pure grace, our work is our play and our play is our work.

But, at any age, being part of a group sometimes requires that we disengage from that which is individually captivating and make a transition to a more social consciousness.

Teachers, visionaries, psychologists, and politicians have long argued about the appropriate balance of work and play, of compliance and freedom at school. Advocates of open classrooms and home schooling might argue that Reesa should have been allowed unlimited time amid swirling leaves. In contrast, those who were successful in moving standards-based education into most public school class-rooms in the early years of the new millennium might counter that the allocation of an hour or more a day for play in first grade cuts into time for reading instruction.

As a teacher in a wonder-centered classroom, my goal is to never sacrifice a moment of wonder. Yet, I know that while I work to pro-tect each moment of awe, protecting every wondrous experience for every child in my care is ultimately impossible. I know too that the best shot at cultivating and protecting sacred moments at school is to entrust each child to teachers who are allowed to make, perhaps, one thousand judgment calls each day, who are given significant freedom in orchestrating the movement of children, dynamically balancing freedom and responsibility in each situation. Thus, the teacher dem-onstrates the dance itself, not just freedom, not just responsibility, but the art of living.

"Be quiet everybody."

I recognized the gentle but firm tone of Rebecca's voice even be-fore I left Reesa at her locker and entered our classroom. This petite, blond second grader, the girl who had once asked in first grade what makes atoms stick together had, as usual, taken over in my absence.

Thomas and Evan, first graders seated in the last row, did not chat, but rather, bent over desks covered with paper and crayons and continued the work we had began earlier. I was surprised to see that Philip, who was usually part of this task-oriented team, sat behind an empty desk, attentive, but not working. Nearby, Galen, a first grader, and Nellie and Jamie, second graders, noticed my arrival, stilled their red, corduroy beanbags, plopped them into a basket, and giggled to-ward their desks.

I had not reprimanded Reesa, but she appeared to be chastising herself as she entered the room with an embarrassed look and hunched silently into her chair. I smiled reassuringly at her, but she stared disconsolately out the window. Again, I was torn between taking a moment with my distressed sheep or caring for the whole flock. The noise level in the room increased. This time I chose the flock.

I considered adding my voice to Rebecca's plea for order, but, instead, I reached for the small wooden recorder that rested on the blackboard ledge. The second graders, who had been my pupils for more than a year, were very familiar with the routine I used to smooth our transitions, the ritual that graced us with a melodious, tranquil interlude instead of a shrill demand for peace.

The idea was that I would play a short melody and that the class would have a few moments to find their seats, to stop talking and to face me, ready to begin our lesson by the time I reached the last note.

The first graders were still learning this routine, except, of course, for Thomas, Evan, and Philip. Their constant vigilance meant they were always ready for the next activity, and they did not need such reminders.

Bringing the recorder to my lips, I glanced toward Philip. The top of his desk was still clear, and he had pushed himself back. He sat perched on the edge of his chair.

Unexpectedly, as I played the first note, he leaped to his feet and began to race full speed across the back of the room.

Everyone, even Thomas and Evan, who put their crayons down, tracked Philip as he thundered around the perimeter of the room while I continued to play my tune. The kids understood what he was up to before I did. Philip had transformed my technique for a mellow transition into a game, a race against the tune clock, a moment of dramatic suspense. Philip tore around the last corner as I leaned into my last musical phrase. Reaching his place, he grabbed his chair and sat down, pulling himself tightly toward the desk, where he folded his hands, looked up at me brightly and grinned in proud victory as I played the last note.

The tension broke and I laughed. Philip laughed. We all laughed. Even Thomas, Rebecca, and Evan let go of their seriousness and laughed. Reesa laughed too until happy tears rolled down her cheeks.

Noticing Reesa's reaction to Philip's antics, I realized that he had done more, much more, than provide the class with a humorous interlude. He had given Reesa what I could not, the warm embrace of laughter at an embarrassing moment. And, his intense and comical attention to the deadline defined by the tune gently raised her awareness of expectations in the new world of first grade.

Philip had given me something too. He had helped me to see that I was not, as I had feared, entering a year of endless choices in which I would feel that I had failed either the whole class or one of the students in it. Philip had lifted Reesa's spirits and her consciousness in a way I could not. And he helped me realize that it was not solely up to me to meet the needs of my children. I would, of course, continue to try to support all of my students and each of my students. But, now, I saw that, in ways beyond their intention or their understanding, and in ways that would fill in the gaps in what I could provide, my kids would take care of each other too.

5

Listening

Our rightful place as educators is to be removers of hindrances....each child in every age brings something new to the world from divine regions, and it is our task as educators to remove bodily and physical obstacles out of his way; to remove hindrances so that his spirit may enter in full freedom into life.

—Rudolf Steiner

WE WEREN'T in a bedroom anymore. Our new classroom in the big, brick school building had real slate blackboards, high ceilings with suspended fluorescent lights, a brown and white linoleum tile floor, and expanses of tall, paned windows. This afternoon, however, it looked more like a refugee camp than a schoolroom.

A makeshift tent city sprawled from my desk at the far end of the room to my rocking chair, where I now sat, near the door. Sheets and blankets, draped over desks and chairs, sheltered wiggling, whispering occupants who were, in theory, preparing for rest and story time.

Two gnome-like faces popped up through the canopy. "Can we go the bathroom?" they asked simultaneously. I nodded, placing a finger over my lips to remind them that it was quiet time. As they disappeared from the room, Megan, a curly haired first grader, crawled out from her tent and whispered in my ear, "Can I go to the bathroom?" "Not yet," I whispered, wanting to avoid a convention in the lavatory. "Wait until Nellie and Cathy get back."

She ignored me and tiptoed toward the door just as if I had given her permission to leave the room. To avoid speaking with a loud voice, I hopped up, took Megan's hand, and led her back toward my chair.

This time I whispered directly into her ear, "I really mean it. You have to wait until Nellie and Cathy get back." She looked at me curiously as if she had never ignored my original directions. Then, she sat down on the floor and picked up the picture book I planned to read to the class.

Megan turned pages in the book while I considered what I would tell her parents the next day at our parent-teacher conference. I knew I would say that she was a cheerful child who played happily with her friends at recess and that she learned letters and numbers, dances, and poems with ease.

Megan stood as she saw Nellie and Cathy return. She smiled at me and I nodded my permission to leave the room.

How, I wondered, would I tell her parents that I was quite concerned because Megan often didn't listen to me. While Megan did whatever I expected the whole group to do, sing, draw, put on coats, line up for recess, she often turned a deaf ear to my direct, personal requests. Other children were eager to help pass out paper or scissors, but Megan often ignored my requests for help. If I called her to me at recess, she sometimes ran in the other direction. And, as I had just seen, if I told her not to leave the room, she sometimes attempted to leave anyway.

"Whispering time is over," I said in a soft voice. I began to hum the lullaby that signaled the beginning of quiet time. Megan tiptoed into the room while I finished the tune, crawled into her tent and grinned conspiratorially at Ellie, her best friend.

Ellie saw me looking. Megan followed her gaze, then quickly pulled the sheet over the opening into their private cave. Intermittent soft giggles bubbled from their hideaway.

Nearby, Reesa lay on a folded blanket holding a worn teddy bear. She rolled to her side and laid the bear next to her on her pillow as if she were a mother laying her baby down for a nap. Closing her eyes and breathing deeply she showed her teddy that she wanted him to go to sleep now. Then she opened her eyes and pulled the little bear closer. She smiled at him, a warm comforting smile, and whispered into his fuzzy little ear. Reesa seemed to have no awareness that I was watching her, that she was one of nineteen children in a chaotic jumble of makeshift tents. Reesa's entire world at that moment was a teddy bear nursery where she was the mommy and teddy her dear baby.

Now the giggles from Megan and Ellie's quarters escalated into full-blown peals of laughter. Megan peeked out from under the sheet and discovered my disapproving look. She offered me one of those endearing smiles that children who are both clever and cute hope will magically absolve them from guilt. It worked. I returned the requisite adult smile that said, "Yes, you are both cute and forgiven, but, now, you must be quiet."

Then, as Megan ducked quietly into her hideaway, I observed Reesa again, now lying on her back holding her little bear over her head. And I thought about how these two first-grade girls were so alike and, yet, so different.

Reesa was often oblivious to my presence and my requests because she was, in a sense, somewhere else, lost in the golden wonder of swirling leaves or busy as the Mommy in a teddy bear nursery.

Megan ignored me too, but she was not somewhere else. She was here. She could still enter a fantasy world, but it no longer held a grip on her. In so many ways, from lining up at recess to quick completion of work, Megan behaved like the second graders and the oldest first graders. And, compared to Reesa, she was acutely aware of my watchful eye. It was obvious that, even behind the walls of her tent, she knew I was listening. This level of mature awareness led me, regretfully, to the unlikely theory that, when she ignored me, she was doing so on purpose.

My training had suggested that first graders were unlikely to show such a strong tendency to disregard adult direction. I was not expecting to see such acts of outright rebellion until the transformation that would come between each child's ninth and tenth birthdays.

Everyday I watched my first and second graders move along an inevitable journey toward that big change. Dreamy six- and seven-year-olds and purposeful seven- and eight-year-olds lived in a spirit of enthusiastic cooperation that revealed their sense of belonging to our class, to our school, to the universe. Sometimes they disagreed with each other. But only rarely did they disagree with me, their teacher. Habitual acts of disobedience seemed as developmentally unlikely as a natural ability to perform long division.

I expected that in third and fourth grade, when the children were nine and ten years old, with the discovery of separateness, I might see occasional moods of defiance. Then I would respond with a more authoritative manner in my teaching, with a curriculum full of stories chosen to help children navigate their mid-childhood crisis.

If Megan had been a second grader I might have seen her as a bit precocious. In our culture there is a tendency to view precociousness in a favorable light, to think that to be ahead of others in development is to be closer to winning a race for achievement. But, childhood is not a race. It is a journey to be savored, and each phase of that journey is a special place with its own wonders, not to be missed.

So, the idea that Megan seemed far ahead in her voyage through the ages of childhood both concerned me and seemed impossible. After all, she was only a first grader, just turning seven. The way she appeared to intentionally ignore my requests made no sense at all.

Loud whispering at the far end of tent city jolted me from my contemplations. I softly sang the song I used to remind the class to remain quiet and made a mental note to return to this puzzle later.

I opened the picture book and said; "Now it is time for our story."

I met Megan's parents, Gloria and Richard, in the classroom the next day after school. I showed them her beautiful drawings and her careful writing. We looked together at the huge, colorful single integers that filled whole pages. I told them Megan interacted appropriately with classmates and usually did what was expected of the whole group.

Then I took a deep breath and began to steer the conversation in a new direction. "I think Megan has a real independent streak," I said.

Richard nodded, "Oh, we sure know that Megan is her own person." Gloria laughed, "Sometimes I think Megan is a little adult. She has her own opinions and doesn't always listen to what we say."

"It's the same at school," I said, relieved that we were all seeing the same thing about Megan. "Often, when I ask her to do things that other children enjoy, such as collect the crayons or paper, she just ignores me. Sometimes first graders are like that, a bit like kindergartners, in their own little worlds. But I am puzzled because Megan seems, in so many ways, to be one of the children who have let go of kindergarten. Sometimes I feel like Megan doesn't even hear me."

The room was silent while Gloria and Richard took this all in. The heating pipes groaned and the windowpanes rattled.

"Maybe she doesn't." Richard said.

I looked at him with a quizzical expression.

"I mean," he continued, "maybe she actually doesn't hear you. Maybe something is wrong with her hearing."

This was a possibility I had not considered. "It's certainly worth looking into," I said.

Gloria looked serious. "Megan is due for a doctor's visit. I'll make it soon and we'll get her hearing checked."

❦

Soon I had a sense that Megan's dad was onto something. In the days after our conference, I was careful to speak loudly and clearly to Megan and to address her only when I saw that she was looking at me. It seemed to make a difference.

So, I was not surprised when Gloria stepped into the empty classroom early on the morning after the doctor's appointment. Her eyes were wide in amazement as she said, "Richard was right. I took Megan to her pediatrician and he found that her ears were packed full of earwax. He said he was surprised she could hear at all. He cleaned it all out and said we should watch it because some people just make a lot of earwax. I think you'll see a difference in Megan. We are already seeing some changes at home. She seems more tuned in. Poor kid, here we were all thinking she ignored us on purpose when really she just couldn't hear."

I was relieved to know that Megan had not somehow, as a first grader, jumped ahead to a developmental stage that she should enter in third grade, that she would have time to enjoy the stage of imaginative wonder that is part of the special territory of the seven-year-old. I cringed when I thought how easy it would have been to perceive Megan as a naughty, willful child. How easy it would have been to go down the road of lectures and punishments designed to teach her to be more attentive. I shuddered when I considered that perhaps, someday, without the help of a father's intuition, I would make the mistake of reading something as misbehavior that was really only a sign of a child needing help. I also thought with chagrin about stories, lessons, and sublime conversations she had likely missed or only partially heard.

Working with wonder is not only about providing inspiring lessons and supporting the class and the individuals in it as they make connections with that which is new and amazing. The most basic level of work of parents and teachers involves helping students be physically, emotionally, and intellectually ready to participate. Steven had needed a bit of support in the form or a story to remain emotionally open and positive. Megan needed relatively minor, yet highly important, help from a doctor to be physically able to hear and therefore to fully participate.

Gloria took her cue to leave from the sounds of clanging of lockers and a tumult of voices approaching the door. I shook hands with each child at the threshold and we settled quickly into main lesson. We sang songs, recited poems, and played number games.

Then it was time to pass out the Main Lesson books, big books of white drawing paper that the students filled with their daily work. I walked behind the rows of children seated at desks to the shelves in back of the room and spoke softly from a place where Megan could not see me. "Megan, would you please come help me pass out our books?"

Megan hopped out of her chair and turned to face me with a big smile. She said nothing, but, as she walked toward me, her shining eyes told me that, ever so gently, a silken veil had been lifted and that now the true Megan could be seen. She scooped up a big pile of the heavy books and began showing off her reading skills by calling out her classmates' names printed on the covers. It was clear that she was glad to help.

6

Resilience

*The world is not comprehensible, but it is embraceable: through
the embracing of one of its beings.*

—Martin Buber

PHILIP RACED up the hill shouting, "Mrs. Allsup, Marc and Jonah are fighting."

It was impossible, I thought, while barreling down the slope behind Philip that these two peace-loving boys could be fighting with each other. But, it was also impossible that Philip could make up such a preposterous story and deliver it in such distress.

Marc's smile lit our classroom from our good morning handshake to our closing song and drew his classmates toward him, like moths fluttering toward a light. A gentle boy, I had never seen him in an argument, let alone a fight.

And, I thought, as I neared a cluster of children by the fence, Jonah would not have been one to provoke Marc. He was gregarious, a walking hug, the first to greet any visitor to our classroom, young or old.

Yet, there they were, two of the tallest first graders, their blond and brown hair visible at the center of the strangely passive group. It appeared that Philip was right. They were actually pushing and shoving each other.

But, as I stepped inside the ring of onlookers, I saw what was happening. Marc and Jonah gripped each other's hands as they had seen the fifth graders do in physical education class in an activity modeled after a form of wrestling used in ancient Greece. Approaching the two boys, I saw that there was no animosity between them. Marc noticed me and, continuing to strain against Jonah, flashed a winning grin that lit his flushed face.

I smiled too, relieved that nobody was being hurt in body or in soul, relieved that I was right about the character of these two sweet boys.

"Hey guys," I said, catching my breath, "Let's stop for a minute."

Jonah and Marc dropped hands. Jonah said, "Can't we practice Greek wrestling?"

Marc's smile grew wide and his eyes widened, "Please?"

"You know, I continued, even the fifth graders don't get to practice until they know all the rules." I looked Marc, then Jonah in the eye. "It's important that a teacher watch while you do this. The fifth graders always have a teacher standing right next to them. I'm not out here at every recess." I slowed my speech and looked directly at Marc then Jonah, "so you will have to ask a teacher to help you if you want to practice again."

Marc and Jonah nodded seriously.

I showed the boys the proper grip and explained that they were not to push against each other with their chests or backs, only their hands. I reminded them that the idea is not to push the other person over, but to push him outside of a circle scratched into the dirt.

Then they grabbed hands at my signal and leaned into each other. First Jonah, the heavier of the two, had the advantage. Then Marc summoned his strength and a disarming smile and forced Jonah to hobble backwards. Back and forth, they stumbled until their arms grew tired and they began to lean on each other chest to chest.

"Hold it guys." I said, stepping forward and touching each boy gently on the shoulder.

They dropped hands and stepped apart.

"I know," said Jonah, "no pushing with our chests."

"That's right, hands only." I reminded them as the melodious voice of a teacher called, "line up, line up."

Marc smiled at Jonah as he turned to jog up the gentle hill. I picked up speed to join them, and then slowed when I realized that my legs hurt. I suddenly felt very tired.

By lunch, I felt achy, tired, and feverish and, convinced that I had the flu, managed to find a substitute and headed toward home.

And, so, I was not at school when Jonah and Marc tried the Greek wrestling again at the next recess and did not ask a teacher to help. That evening a colleague called to tell me that Jonah had fallen on top of Marc's leg. There had been suspicion of a break so the leg had been splinted and Marc had been taken to the hospital for x-rays.

I called Marc's mother. Her voice was tired but calm, so I was not prepared for what she would say. "We're just getting in from the hospital now. It's broken all right, a bad break too. The doctor thinks he'll be out of school for at least a week, maybe two. He's already called Jonah to tell him it wasn't his fault."

I lay awake through much of that Friday night, still aching with my flu symptoms, but aching more for Marc, wishing I had outlawed the wrestling practice, wishing that I had been at school to comfort him after this strange accident.

By morning, unexpectedly, my flu symptoms were gone and I drove south along the bay to Marc's home. As I drove, I wished I could somehow lift Marc's pain. A young child's pain elicits a special sympathy from adults who remember their own childhood sensitivity. All little children are completely immersed in sense impressions, both pleasure and pain. Unlike adults or older children, they cannot create barriers to experience. The consciousness that opens young children so completely to wonder also causes them to be unable to create inner defenses against pain.

I remembered hearing in teacher training that young children soak up sense impressions like a sponge. This is a reason for protecting young children from many of the sensory intrusions that we adults accept as part of modern life, and this is why we should surround our youngest students with beauty.

I thought about the primacy of sensory awareness in my students, Sally contemplating her apple, Reesa lost in a rain shower of golden leaves. I remembered experiences from my own childhood, a heap of fuzzy yellow dandelions in my lap and splitting the light green milky stems with my fingernails to weave a rope brighter than sunshine. My world became living sunshine. The world sometimes became fresh bread, apple blossoms, soft pajamas, hot beach sand. Once, I accidentally stuck my thumb under a shovel as my brother jammed it into the earth. Then, for a day, the world became my throbbing, swollen thumb.

Marc's world would be a sore leg, encased in a cast from ankle to thigh, his pain and immobility far greater than I experienced with my injured thumb. The flood of sensory impressions would, I expected, wash away Marc's smile for weeks, perhaps months. Then it might be a different smile, older, less frequent, more guarded. These were my thoughts as I pulled into the driveway at Marc's house.

I saw Marc before he noticed me. He was propped up on pillows in his parents' big bed, his right leg, wrapped in a thick white cast, jutting out before him. His face was flushed and tired. He looked tired, small, defeated, and old.

Then he turned and he saw me. "Hi, Marc," I said softly.

"Hi," he said in a soft voice that carried pain and exhaustion.

Then Marc began to teach me something that I will never forget.

Slowly, a gentle smile kindled across his face, gathered strength and spread until it briefly lit his light blue eyes.

His face still bore the signs of unremitting pain, but through all of that, his light burned brightly. It was as if he was saying to me, "Yes I hurt, but that has nothing to do with the fact that I am happy to see you."

Marc arrived at school two weeks later in a candy-red wheelchair. His classmates thronged around him, thrilled to have him back in school, thrilled to drink in his infectious grin, thrilled to offer help, especially if it involved pushing Marc in the wheelchair.

"You pushed the wheelchair when he got to school. It's my turn"

"I claim recess."

"I claim the second recess."

"No fair! The second recess is longer."

Marc beamed pontifically at his classmates swarming around him. His broken leg, encased in a hard cast stuck straight out in front of him. It was still tender, even with the protection of the cast, and I sensed we were seconds away from a painful bump.

"Hold on guys," I said in my loud teacher voice. "Let's sit at our desks, then we can figure out how to take turns helping Marc."

The children settled in quickly, then looked at me expectantly. "I think it will work best if everyone gets a turn for a whole day to help Marc." I wrote Evan's name at the upper right hand corner of the blackboard.

"I see Evan helped Marc first today, so he can be Marc's special helper for the rest of the day. I will put up a list of all the names in the class so each of you will know when it will be your day to help Marc."

So, from late October through December the children took turns pushing Marc's chair, hauling his things and helping him at his locker.

At Christmas time we memorized "'Twas the Night Before Christmas" by Clement Moore, then I gave everyone a part so we could act it out. Marc was St. Nick on his red, wheeled sleigh. He grasped two jump ropes and Comet and Cupid and Donner and Blitzen and their kin pulled him around the classroom in his red wheelchair and whirled his smile into peals of infectious laughter. Never was there a more jolly young elf.

This was a high point in Marc's school experience during his recuperation, but there were low points too. At first, there were the winces from accidental bumps. Then came a time when sitting in a wheelchair watching others play was too hard and he chose to stay inside and draw or look at a book. Finally, after the Christmas vacation, there was the frustration of a longer than expected transition from wheelchair to crutches to independent walking.

But, through it all, alongside the pain, the winces, and the frustration, lived the spark of delight that shone whenever he was in the close companionship of his friends. I could not know it then, but I was beginning to see a part of Marc's character that would endear him to his classmates for years to come.

It is a mystery how Marc came to appreciate the people in his life so deeply and so early. We each have our predilections toward finding wonder in certain types of experiences and some children show these tendencies at an early age. More than most children, indeed, more than most adults, Marc appeared to find wonder in people. This awed appreciation for friends, family, teachers is what lit his luminous smile. And because he found wonder in everyone, Marc attracted fond regard from all.

The most basic level of working with wonder involves helping children be physically, emotionally, and intellectually capable of interacting with all that comes to them in a school day. Over my first year and a half as a teacher, I had already found myself working on a problem with hearing and a threat to self-confidence. Now I expected that after Marc's accident, I would take on the task of supporting the rebuilding of a sense of wonder that had been eclipsed by his pain and immobility. I had been wrong. Marc had developed such a deep habit of delight in other people that he was able on his own to retain his sense of wonder throughout his ordeal. It was not just that he seemed to come out of the other side of this trial with his inner life intact; he had gone through each day of this challenge with remarkable resilience.

Adults can create an inner buffer that protects them from the depth of pain experienced by children. Surprisingly, at six years old, Marc already showed signs of creating such a wall of inner protection. In the moments when he experienced delight in people, his sense of wonder appeared, at least momentarily, to serve as a barrier to his intense six-year-old awareness of his pain.

Someday, I would be able to look at each child in the class and think of an ability or an understanding that surpassed my own. Thomas would have better handwriting. Evan would become a better artist. Rebecca would be quicker than I with the tactful comment that would bring peace to an escalating argument. Reesa would surprise me with her perception of deep truths in ancient stories, truths that eluded me until she shared her insight.

In the fall and winter of his first grade year, Marc demonstrated with each warm, wonder-filled smile that we can stand apart from our difficulties and showed me that my children would teach me as much or more than I would teach them.

7

Gratitude

...the reality of the spiritual world was as certain to me as that of the physical. I felt the need, however, for a sort of justification for this assumption.

—Rudolf Steiner

AT SEVEN IN THE MORNING the air was damp, not a hot, heavy summer mugginess, but the brisk dampness that portends the life of spring. I drank in that cool dampness, and that spring feeling that everything is new, and all things are possible, as we descended through a pine-needled path, flanked by throngs of purple lady slippers. My eleven-year-old daughter, Nora, and I were headed toward the wobbly concrete bridge that spans the neck between two of the four ponds that are the namesake of the Four Ponds Conservation Area.

We had come here often on Saturday morning family hikes, but this was a school day and I was here to create a lesson plan. My task was to imagine a story that took place in these woods, by these ponds. I planned to tell the class the story at the start of the school day and then to return to the woods with the children and five chaperones.

The story was about a fairy who flitted through the woods. It was meant to lead the children on a journey of discovery. The children would remember clues from the story about the fairy's journey and these clues would lead them, with no adult assistance, between the budding trees, over the concrete bridge, by the mossy shore, over the wooden bridge, through a narrow, bushy tunnel between two ponds, up and down a sandy road, along a skunk cabbage studded marsh, back over the wooden bridge and up the hill to the parking lot.

53

Like any treasure hunt it would be most exciting if the clues were not easy give-aways, but challenging puzzles. I looked for clues that would trigger an awareness of the buds on the bushes, the shapes and colors of the trees, the patterns of grass and moss, rocks, and puddles.

We paused at an intersection of paths. Turning left would lead down the muddy path toward the bridge. Turning right would lead toward higher ground. I looked for a clue for a left turn. Imagining a little fairy hovering over the path, I saw that she would be attracted to a tiny, soft, green forest just to the left. It was a pleasant glade perched a foot higher than the sticky mud that could soil a fairy's delicate wings. The little, round forest had fuzzy trees only an inch tall, a plush green carpet and an acorn for a seat.

I pulled a small notebook out of my pocket and noted the glade. Smiling, I planned my description of the fairy's haven, a description that would leave out the obvious, give-away words: mossy stump. Then, I popped the notebook in my pocket, skirted the mud by tottering on the grassy edge of the path, and met Nora at the concrete bridge.

The bridge, a six-inch thick slab of concrete, rested about a foot above the confluence of the ponds. Nora stood in the middle, legs apart, shifting her weight from one side to the other. Calunk. Calunk. Calunk. Her motion was just enough to make the concrete wobble. There was something satisfying about the deep clunking sound and its faint echo across the ponds. And there was something pleasing about our ritual of making the clunking noise every time we passed over this bridge. I thought about a way to work the wobble of the bridge into the story. Perhaps the fairy would listen for the clunking noise as a sign that people were approaching. Then I noted a clue that would hint at another left turn and we headed down the path along the tree-lined pond.

"Mom, you have to see this," called Nora excitedly, breaking our silence of many minutes. She gazed at a shining, dew-dropped strand of a spider's web that crossed the path. The center part of the strand glistened with the dew and appeared to hang mid-air with no support at either end.

We ducked carefully beneath the glistening strand to observe it from the other side. We peered at it from above, from below, from close up and at a distance. Still, we could see no supporting threads connecting this taught filament to the branches at either side of the path.

I stared at the magic before us. I knew that this was not magic, that we were looking at an optical illusion and, at the same time, I knew that this was the best magic of all. No human conjurer had a hand in this. The delicate filament defied gravity. It was held up by something invisible.

"I think we can't see the ends of the web because they are in shadow," speculated Nora as she bobbed up and down in search of a view that would reveal the invisible supporting pieces of the strands.

"I suspect you are right," I said "but it still seems magical to me."

In my mind I hopped back and forth between the magic-filled wonder of the seven-year-old children who I would soon greet at school and the reality-based wonder that is firmly rooted in an eleven-year-old who wants to know the truth, the facts behind the apparition.

Both the seven-year-old and the eleven-year-old would be awed by a strand hanging in space with no visible support, but the seven-year-old would be more likely to accept this as simply amazing without need of explanation, or, if explanation is needed, the handiwork of fairies or wizards.

The wonder of an eleven-year-old is not diminished by eschewing

magic, but, rather, wonder at this age is strengthened by understanding how something works. Adults also find wonder in realistic explanations and it is natural to want to share our enthusiasm for the
real world with children, even very young children. Often, however,
it is best to wait, to support the open-eyed observation and innocent
wonder that needs no explanation, to facilitate the imaginative thinking of the seven-year-old that will develop into the perceptive prob-
ing of the eleven-year-old.

I looked across the tranquil pond at the forested hill on the other side
and realized that we had a long walk ahead of us before we would
climb that hill to the parking lot and then drive to school, and that
the entire journey had to be completed by eight o'clock. We took a last
look at the glistening strand, still suspended in mid-air by its illusive,
invisible support, and hiked down the path along the mossy bank. A
light breeze ruffled the pond and I wondered whether branches sway-
ing in the wind had already snapped the delicate filament.

As we walked, I pulled out my notebook again and again to jot
down clues to weave into the story. We crossed the wooden bridge,
passed through the bushy tunnel and came to the wide sandy road. We
were far from the magical strand now, but it was not far from my mind.

"Invisible support." I kept repeating these words to myself. "Invisible support." I thought about how we could not exist without the
support of so many people and things that were usually out of sight,
far from our awareness: the friends and family that care about us, the
farmers who grow our food, the sunlight and the oxygen we breathe.
Our strength, our breath, our thoughts and feelings were held up by
invisible strands.

And what about invisible support from realms less apparent, the realms of the spiritual world that Rudolf Steiner said stood behind our lives and our teaching. My own connection to this invisible world of the spirit was rooted in a perception of God as a mysterious entity or force that cannot be understood, a distant entity who was probably not interested in the details of my life.

Steiner saw a more personal heaven, with a panoply of angels and departed souls listening to our prayers and meditations. I had been wrestling with his vision for many years and now his understanding of the spiritual world came to mind as I reflected on the web suspended by mysterious forces.

My willingness to give credence to this host of imperceptible supporters was tentative at best. Maybe my grandmother watched over me from heaven. Maybe someone was listening to my evening meditations on the children in my class. Maybe these spiritual beings could help guide my teaching, or maybe the meditations only helped me reach into my own subconscious.

I recalled looking at the glistening strand and thinking, "Of course there is something real holding this up. I can't see it and I don't understand the optical illusion, but I know the web continues unseen." And, with that thought, came an image of me as the visible piece of web and the hidden connecting strands as invisible spiritual helpers.

Then I repeated these words to myself again, this time thinking of invisible support from the spiritual world, "I can't see it and I don't understand it, but I know the web continues unseen."

And with that thought, that image, every "maybe" changed into a bold "yes" and I experienced a calming and reassuring, yet electric, sensation. It was like the surprising feeling of floating, floating for the first time as a six-year-old at the beach. One moment I am standing waist deep, looking at the horizon, then I am floating on my back, looking at the sky.

Only this time it wasn't water and it wasn't my body that was unexpectedly suspended above firm ground, it was something inside myself. I felt a powerful rush of confident energy and a sea of very personal support as if my grandmother and all the grandparents of all time had come together to carry me on invisible wings. These wings lifted me over the wooden bridge and swooped me up the hill and toward the car.

My fairy story fell together effortlessly as we drove to school and parked by the baseball field. "See you after school, Pumpkin. Thanks for getting up early this morning and for finding that awesome spider's web," I said to Nora as we walked toward the school building.

I floated into the school and was more aware than ever of the massive presence of this old brick building. Entering my classroom, the solid maple floor, the dense slate blackboards and the heavy maple desks balanced my airy feeling and helped to bring me down to earth. Feeling both rooted to the substantial brick building and uplifted by the electricity of discovery, I soon faced eighteen children, four parents and another teacher.

I wanted to share this electricity, to share my wonder at the marvel we had seen and the marvel I had felt. And, I wanted to convey not only the marvels, but the metaphor. Last year, it had been Helen who sparked a conversation about invisible connections in time and space, about the oneness of all things. Today, it would be my turn to remind my class of the hidden continuum that binds all of creation.

I wanted to place before my students a lesson that could become a science lesson, or a religion lesson, but would become neither today. Today, it would be a lesson in the wonder that lies beneath both. I looked at the parents standing in front of the tall bank of windows and saw at that moment how to share the metaphor, how to share my own amazement in a way that would be appropriate for my first graders.

"Early this morning I walked the path we will follow today at Four Ponds. I could tell that no one, except someone very small like a fairy, had walked the path before us. Delicately hanging above the path were webs, sometimes just individual strands spun by spiders. Some of the strands glistened with dew. One of the strands was quite amazing. It was covered by shining droplets and it appeared to float over the path, unconnected to anything. I looked from every angle and I could not see how the strand was held up. Perhaps a fairy could see how it was supported but I could not."

"You may not understand this now, but I think you will understand it when you are older. Many times in your life, you will come across things that are like that strand, things that are held up by something invisible. As I look at all of you here today and look at the four parents who have joined us, I think about all the parents who are at work or at home today. They take good care of you. They give you a warm bed in a nice house. They make your lunch and bring you to school. You could not be here today without them, yet we cannot see them right now. Right now, to us, they are invisible, yet they are very real. They are like the invisible part of the strand left by the spider. All of those parents and so many other invisible things support us as we begin this day. We can't see the farmers who grow our food. We can't see the well beneath the earth that gives us water. We can't see the air we breathe. But all these things help us and support us."

I could not have imagined this part of the lesson when I planned it the night before. It was about invisible support, and at the same time I wondered whether the lesson itself had been given to me by the invisible supporters who guide my teaching.

I paused and told my fairy story. Then I orchestrated bathroom trips and reminded everyone about coats, hats, backpacks, and snacks. Chaperones found their appointed children and we drove in a caravan to the conservation area where small groups of children remembered the story and its clues well enough to lead the adults on the fairy's journey.

I smiled as I watched Marc mingling with his group before beginning our hike. It was good to see him without a wheelchair, without crutches, free to walk through the spring woods.

It was like watching an Easter egg hunt. I paused before each intersection and waited for my group of children to notice the clue from the story.

"Look!" shouted Reesa as she ran over to the mossy stump. "I think this is where the fairy rested!" She bent over and ran her hand over the soft moss. "It was on this stump. See, the green carpet is this moss, and here is the acorn she sat on."

Evan ran up and surveyed the fairy's haunt. Then he stepped back and pointed down the path toward the pond. "And there is the mud that she didn't want to get on her wings, yuck!"

It would have been wonderful for the children to find a magical floating strand. Yet, as we made our way through the woods, no such magic appeared. The delicate strand had gone the way of all ephemeral apparitions that are reported by observers and never seen again. I had prepared the children to not rediscover our early morning find by saying that a squirrel or a bird or the branches shaking in the wind would probably break the thin thread before we arrived. But, while they found no floating strands, they did travel through a path of magic and discovery as they followed a delicate fairy that flitted through the woods.

That evening, as I began my review of the day, I remembered

our woodland journey. Of course the story of the fairy was meant to awaken powers of observation, to encourage the careful looking that leads to noticing the details of the landscape. While a visit to the forest with only one or two or three children can lead to an awareness of moss and rocks, carpets of pine needles, and protection from tall, arching pines, children in a big group are often most aware of their group dynamic. I had hoped that the fairy's journey would tug the children's awareness away from joking with a classmate and into communion with the forest. Reviewing memories of our morning, I saw that my strategy had worked.

The class had been able to let go of their chatting and they had easily drifted into the mood of organic wonder that we experience in nature. I pictured Reesa's sunlit face as she stroked the soft moss, Evan's scrunched up face as he beheld the yucky mud, the dynamic silence as children looked for clues, as they gazed intently at branches, at rocks, at lady slippers, and then suddenly proclaimed their discoveries. In the classroom, I had to work at creating a setting for wonder, but in the woods all a teacher needs to do is to find a way to loosen the social grip of the class and allow nature to be the teacher.

And, I reflected on my own discovery. This time it was not my young students who had awakened my awareness of a hidden web that binds all things. Today, with Nora, I had found the portal to such an epiphany under a bush in the damp spring woods.

Now, a stream of questions, questions without answers, poured through my soul. Could Steiner be right? Could the powerful sense of connection to something supportive in the spiritual world be more than my imagination? Might I learn to connect to this spiritual source at will, to stay connected, to become a funnel for divine inspiration for myself and my students?

I knew that Rudolf Steiner encouraged students of the spirit to be more than believers. He wanted us to subject our inner experiences to objective thought, to ask questions and to seek answers that made sense to us. I remembered the cryptic answer of a professor in teacher training when I shared a list of questions about Steiner's teachings, "Live with these questions," he advised.

It was time to begin my evening meditations on each child in the class. I closed my eyes, sank into a deep silence and began to call forth the image of each child. It was like any other evening when pictures of the children settled one at a time in my mind.

Only, this time, before I opened my eyes, there came, unbidden, one more question, which I addressed to the spiritual beings who might guide my teaching, the invisible supporters I had felt in the woods:

"Are you there?"

8

Perspective

Educators, parents, teachers will all have learned from experience that what you say is not decisive. What you are, and what you do, play a far greater role. And it is this above all which gives weight to the words you may say later.
—Jens Bjørneboe

REBECCA PICKED UP the green pencil that lay in the aisle. "Whose pencil is this?" She asked.

Jonah took the pencil from Rebecca's hand, saying, "It's mine."

"It is not!" Reesa exclaimed, jumping to her feet and reaching toward Jonah, intending to snatch it away. I intervened by stepping between the two with my hand outstretched. Jonah put the pencil on my palm.

We were only a month into our second and third grade year and already it seemed that moving between two students to negotiate a dispute had become a familiar routine.

"Seems like you both think this belongs to you," I said.

Reesa held up her pencil box, pointing to the space meant for the green pencil. "Look" she said, "my green pencil is missing."

Jonah held up his pencil box. "Mine is too," he said, in a sharp tone that surprised me. "And," he continued, "Rebecca found the pencil closer to my chair."

Fearing that her case for the pencil might be lost on the basis of proximity, Reesa's eyes suddenly filled with tears.

"I am sure we can get an extra green pencil." I said, hoping to calm unexpectedly strong emotions, hoping that either Jonah or

Reesa would offer to take the new pencil and concede the disputed pencil to the other student.

Instead, Jonah said, "But I want my own pencil."

Reesa said, "It's not yours, it's mine. Look, it has my teeth marks on it."

I walked over to my desk and put the pencil on it. "It's impossible for me to know who this really belongs to," I said, "So it would be unfair to give it to either of you right now."

I paused, an opening for someone to concede the pencil. Instead, Cathy joined in, "I know it's Reesa's," she said. She always chews on her pencils and leaves marks like that."

"So," I continued, before anyone else could offer an opinion and escalate this minor dispute into a class-wide quarrel, "I will keep the pencil myself."

I stood behind my desk, knowing I could not just leave it at that. This dispute and the ones that I had already refereed this year, and the ones that no doubt would follow, were to be expected now that we had turned the corner into second and third grade. In first grade inner doors to wonder lured children into a dreamland. This meant that I, an adult with goals and a schedule to keep, lived with a theme of patient waiting, waiting for dreamy first grade children to stop talking and listen, to finish snack, to pass out main lesson books, put away crayons, zip jackets, tie shoes, to wend their way up the long recess hill. Now the waiting was over.

My kids could now keep crayons and pencils well organized. Everyone could finish lunch, don jackets, and get out to play in short order. And, even Reesa could let go of her play and line up quickly at the end of recess.

But this ability to focus, this burgeoning capacity for moving through tasks toward a goal, had its price. Second graders could be so goal oriented, so taken with their own personal trajectories that they often bumped into their classmates both physically and emotionally.

I knew that this year would bring a stream of incidents like this one and that it was my job to somehow teach my students how to move through life more like dancers and less like bumper cars.

Rudolf Steiner, the founder of Waldorf education, had an uncanny ability to understand the inner reality of children at each age and stage. His pedagogical recipes were carefully designed to meet the needs of children at each grade level.

For second graders he suggested a soup of two types of tales, stories of saints and stories of sinners. Our year would be full of role models of generous people, from Saint Francis to Mother Theresa. And we would laugh at the greed and self-centered antics in Aesop's fables, recognizing deeply that we were seeing ourselves.

But, right now, I didn't have a saint story or a fable up my sleeve. And, as I stared over the heads of my class toward the window, I realized that the soul food of stories would not be enough to carry us through this year. Just as first grade had called on me to come to an inner place of patience, second grade, and each grade to come, would call on me to find an inner gesture that would meet the needs of the class.

If first grade was about waiting, this year would be about thinking on my feet. While first graders called me to join them in wonder, second graders would sometimes need me to lead them to wonder through wisdom. Unfortunately, at that moment, I did not feel very wise.

The pause before I spoke was long, too long. I looked at the class as if I had something to say only nothing came to mind. No one spoke. Then my gaze fell on the closet door and I smiled.

This time, I was saved. I would hardly have to speak. What I was about to pull out of the closet would do most of the talking.

I walked to the closet. Here, on the top shelf, unknown to the children, rested a plain cardboard box where I stored sentimental memorabilia that I had collected since the beginning of our time together. I pulled the box down and carried it to the front of the room.

"Who remembers this?" I asked, pulling a yellow felt gnome out of the box.

Many voices called out excitedly, "It's Uncle." Uncle, a gnome with a rather unusual name, had been part of our class the previous year and had helped us learn the short vowel sound for the letter "u."

Everyone, even Jonah and Reesa, looked expectantly at the box.

"And what about this?" I asked holding up the playbill from our first grade play.

"It's from our play," said Jamie enthusiastically. His eyes lit up with a reminder of our performance.

"This box has more things that are part of our memories." I said, "We will put things in here until the end of eighth grade, then we will open it and remember all of our years together. Now, since I can't figure out who this pencil belongs to, I am going to put it in the eighth-grade box."

I wrote on a piece of paper, "Reesa and Jonah disagreed about who owned this pencil in second grade." I told the class what I had written, wrapped the paper tightly around the pencil, secured it with a rubber band, and put it in the box.

"I think in eighth grade both of you will probably laugh at this. I expect you will both say, 'you can have that old pencil. It probably wasn't mine anyway.'"

Reesa's eyes opened wide. This was not her first grade dreamy gaze, but a wide awake, intent appearance that was the new face of wonder in a second grader. Jonah's expression was an alert mix of mirth and thoughtfulness. Neither child spoke as I placed the pencil in the box.

"Now," I said, "the box will go back to the top of our closet, and we will go back to our lesson."

Yet, I knew full well as I said it that the most important part of our work, our main lesson today, had already transpired. It had been a brief lesson and an unexpected one, a lesson that would not be complete until we opened the box many years hence.

9

Respect

To educate the whole child, his heart and will must be reached, as well as his mind.
—Rudolf Steiner

"REBECCA, will you be my girlfriend?" Peter, a new second grader, spoke in tone that was casual, but Rebecca's answer conveyed strained patience.

"No I won't. I told you that yesterday. *Please* quit bothering me."

This was not the first time I had overheard such a conversation at recess. The class had been humored for weeks by their new classmate's unrequited fondness for Rebecca, a third grader who had no interest in his attentions.

The next morning I heard a similar conversation before school. This time Peter's voice was pleading. "Please will you be my girlfriend?"

Rebecca replied angrily, "Just stop bothering me!"

This was the first time I had ever heard Rebecca use such a strong tone of voice.

If the two children had been in kindergarten, Rebecca might have agreed to be Peter's girlfriend. Then she might have agreed to marry him and they might have invited the whole class and play-acted a wedding ceremony.

But they were not in kindergarten and Rebecca had reached the age when she knew that courtship was meant for people much older than she. And, for now, the idea of a romantic connection with a boy was just plain yucky.

Peter didn't see it that way at all. His big brother, his teenage idol, was a high school student. Peter didn't see the subtle side of his romantic liaisons. He simply knew that his brother was very cool and that he had found friendship with a female companion he called a girlfriend.

From the perspective of an eight-year-old boy, it didn't seem like such a difficult thing to ask someone to be your girlfriend. And, why not pick a girl who greeted you in a friendly way on your first day in the school, who was liked by all, who was always well-behaved? And, if she did not say, "Sure, I'll be your girlfriend," why not just wait and ask again on another day?

This was the stuff of second grade. Just as Jonah and Reesa had wished to restore a personal sense of order by returning a green pencil to its proper place in a pencil box, Peter wished to find a larger sense of order by securing an abiding connection to Rebecca, a child with a well-established place in the social order of the class. And, just as Reesa and Jonah had not been able to see beyond the pencil to the feelings of a classmate, Peter could not see beyond his wish for a girl-friend to how Rebecca might feel about such a relationship nor could he sense that she would prefer a more natural growth in a friendship.

Rebecca was not able to appreciate the innocence in Peter's re-quests. She was rounding an invisible corner into the territory of third grade. When the class sang, her voice was softer than it once had been. She had once taken on the role of assistant teacher, telling other students how to behave. Now, she was quiet when others mis-behaved. While Rebecca wanted to be increasingly invisible, Peter's attentions increased her visibility in a very embarrassing way.

For the most part, I found that the children in our combined class were able to learn and play together in harmony. But now the boisterous innocence of second grade collided with the dignified self-consciousness of third grade. I began to worry about whether wonder would ever again flow easily through our days and became concerned about my inexperience as I tried to be a midwife of the inner life of eight- and nine-year-old children.

❦

One morning, as we were settling in before the start of Main Lesson, Peter's voice rang through the classroom.

"Who did it? Who put water on my chair?"

I rushed to the scene of the crime where he pointed and said, "Someone poured water on my chair and I almost sat in it!"

The class gathered around and observed, as I did, that sure enough, a puddle lay in the concave center of Peter's wooden chair.

I looked up at our stained ceiling that was known to drip during a heavy rainstorm, "Well, Peter," I said," I don't see any sign of leaking water, so I suppose someone must have put it there."

Thirteen cherubic faces surveyed the six-inch diameter puddle.

"Anyone know who did this?" I asked matter of factly.

An authoritative voice said, "It was Rebecca."

Rebecca had shown only exemplary behavior for over two years, so I dismissed this statement and continued, "Whoever did this can see how upset it has made Peter. Maybe that person thought it was a joke, but now that they know how unhappy Peter is, maybe that person is sorry."

We stood silently around the little puddle.

A small voice said, "I did it." Rebecca blushed and looked at her feet.

Our silence deepened.

Then Jamie laughed aloud and said, "I guess teacher's pet is in trouble now." I shot him a look of disapproval and his smirk vanished.

"Rebecca." I said, "Thank you for telling the truth. First, you need to clean this up, then you and Peter and I will have a talk. Megan, would you please go with Rebecca to get paper towels?"

I needed an activity to buy a little time. "Everyone else, take a few minutes to clean inside your desks." I looked at Thomas and Philip who always kept their desks in perfect order. If your desk is already clean," I told them, "please help a friend."

The room buzzed with activity, a partial screen for a private conversation while I met with Rebecca and Peter at my desk.

"Rebecca, I guess you have something to say to Peter."

"I'm sorry," she said tersely.

"Peter, what do you say?"

He knew the words he was expected to utter.

"I accept your apology," he said, and without pausing, continued, "What are you going to do to her?"

"Well, Peter," I said, "I have to think about that. I am really sorry this happened to you, but I want to talk with Rebecca alone about what she did. Would you mind working on cleaning your desk while we have a private conversation?"

Peter nodded and walked away.

Rebecca's tears flowed down her cheeks. She quickly wiped them away and said, "I know I shouldn't have done it, but he wouldn't listen to me. He just kept bothering me."

I looked pensively into Rebecca's reddened eyes and I remembered her angry tone of voice as she attempted to quell Peter's attentions.

"Rebecca" I said, "I see you don't like it when Peter asks you to be his girlfriend. But there are right ways to deal with problems and wrong ways. I wish you had come to me and told me how upset you were."

Rebecca nodded her head.

I thought about restitution. I usually said to a child who had mis-
behaved, "if you take something away from the class, you have to
give something back. And everyone will benefit from a cleaner classroom. You can stay in from recess and sweep the floor and wash the
blackboard."

Today, though, I had recess duty and could not supervise a student who was in the classroom doing restitution though cleaning. I
considered telling Rebecca she could postpone her community service until the following day, but then I realized that anything less than
immediate consequences would add to the perception that she was,
in fact, teacher's pet.

"I guess I'm going to have to miss recess," Rebecca said, apparently reading my mind.

"That's right," I said, amazed at her easy acceptance of her fate.

"I will be out on the lower grade playground today," I said.

"So I guess I'll be sitting on the steps." She added in a tone that
was surprisingly composed.

From my vantage point midway down the long hill, Rebecca, perched
at the edge of the broad concrete steps, appeared tiny, fragile and very
much alone.

I thought about her two-year stretch of model behavior and I considered her quick confession and her calm acceptance of consequences.

I looked at my watch. Maybe, I thought, considering the fact that
this was a first infraction, missing half of recess was enough. I began
walking up the hill with early parole in mind. But, as I drew closer, I
perceived something I had not noticed. I realized that Rebecca's posture and her demeanor were not fragile at all. There was something
upright and resolute about her carriage, something that said, "Look at

me. I am not teacher's pet. See, I am not perfect after all and I never wanted to be. I can get in trouble just like anyone else and I am tough enough to handle the consequences."

What came to mind was that, perhaps, something good had come of this messy social situation. Perhaps losing recess would dispel the notion that Rebecca held such a lofty, but embarrassing, position in the class.

I was reminded of what the character Pa says in *Little House on the Prairie,* " Out of every great loss comes some small gain."

I also saw that Rebecca, one of my third grade students, was showing signs of being almost nine years old, the age of the great change. Her embarrassment about being called someone's girlfriend, her willingness to break rules in an unprecedented act, her proud bearing on the steps, all pointed to a new consciousness dawning in Rebecca.

So, I changed my mind about parole. I told Rebecca that I truly appreciated her honesty. But, with only a few minutes of recess remaining, I did not let her off.

I walked down the hill, carpeted again in golden leaves. And I remembered Reesa, a year before on a similar day, dancing in the golden splendor, heedless of her responsibilities. This time it was I who had been heedless. Just as Reesa had not noticed a clear call to line up after recess, I had not noticed Rebecca's clear signs of growing frustration.

I should have caught this long ago, I thought. I should have been highly aware that my role as a teacher of eight- and nine-year-olds, it was my job to intervene in challenging social situations. I should have taken the two aside for a conversation. I should have informed their parents of the escalating conflict rooted in differing perspectives. I should have worked at it until Peter calmly accepted that Rebecca would be his friend, but would not be his girlfriend. I should have made it possible for Rebecca to enjoy Peter's company. But I hadn't done any of that, and now Peter felt even less connected to his new class, and Rebecca had committed the only act of misbehavior she would ever have at school.

I was becoming increasingly less hopeful that unexpected, transcendent moments would again grace our days. It wasn't as if we had totally lost a mood of wonder. Our curriculum was rich with color, movement, music, and stories. Yet, the unanticipated moments when the children initiated an exploration in the realm of the sublime were, I thought, a sign of health.

Over the next week I did what I should have done sooner. I spoke with Peter's parents and Rebecca's parents. I explained the differing perspectives that led to their ongoing conflict. And I looked for the right moment to have a conversation with the two children.

It came on a rainy day during indoor recess when our room was alive with children jumping rope, tossing beanbags, and building forts out of cloths and chairs. In the middle of the cacophony, I summoned Peter and Rebecca. We sat together on the carpet.

Peter had stopped asking Rebecca to be his girlfriend, but an icy tension lived between them. Sometimes Peter announced for no apparent reason, "Rebecca doesn't like me."

"Well guys," I said, "I was hoping we could have a little talk about you two being friends."

"Rebecca doesn't like me," Peter said matter of factly. "I never said I didn't like you," Rebecca sounded frustrated and, surprisingly, near tears. I realized that the continuing strain of her unresolved conflict with Peter had been weighing on her. She continued in a softer voice. "I just said I wouldn't be your girlfriend."

"Peter," I said gently, "there is a difference between being a friend and being a girlfriend."

We sat quietly for a moment. Rebecca regained her composure. Then Peter brightened.

"So you'll be my friend?"

"I never said I wasn't your friend."

Peter smiled.

Rebecca rolled her eyes, suppressed a grin, and shook her head.

I smiled and said, "You two still have some time to play. I'm glad you will be friends now."

We had reached a point of resolution. It had come later than I would have wished, but finally the conflict was behind us. I could see that Peter and Rebecca both felt relieved.

I did too.

10

Nurturing

When we practice love, cultivate love, creative forces pour into the world.
—Rudolf Steiner

IT WAS OCTOBER and we had a new classmate. She was tiny and cute and tended to fall asleep during class. She needed lots of attention. Sometimes she cried and I had to stop teaching and hold her on my lap. Nobody minded. Everyone waited patiently while I helped her calm down. Then we went back to our lesson.

Our new classmate was, after all, only a newborn kitten.

Abandoned by her mother outside our living room window, the little feline had become my constant companion. When she wasn't nestling in my hands for a feeding, she curled up on a hot water bottle in a cozy box that sat beside me wherever I went.

Now, while the children ate their snack, the little ball of white fur huddled in my hand. I filled the doll-sized bottle with newborn kitten formula and did the best I could to simulate a mother cat. I stroked the top of her head and waited for the tiny paws to push against my thumb and for the soft pink mouth to open. Tucking the nipple of the two-ounce bottle into the kitten's mouth, I felt her entire diminutive being pulse in the rhythm of feeding.

The children ate too, but their attention was not on their food, but on the little ball of fur snuggled in my hands.

"Mrs. Allsup, when can we hold her?"

I wasn't sure who had said it. I, too, had been watching the kitten.

Now I saw in the eyes of my students that any of them could have uttered this question. Newborn kitten care was not a planned element of my second and third grade curriculum. But, looking at the fervent desire to hold, to help this little creature, I thought I saw a glimmer of the gesture of the saints and other generous people we would study this year and I realized that I had been wrong to doubt whether my kids still retained the perennial yet mysterious source of the stream of wonder that flowed easily when they were first graders.

I saw too that the first lesson would be about restraint, for the survival of this new, young being depended on a time of protection from eager little hands.

"I'm sorry to say that it will still be a few weeks before we can take turns holding her," I said. "We have to wait until her eyes open and she begins to move around more in her box."

It was a lot to ask, this degree of patience, yet nobody complained.

I smiled and said, "We can't take turns holding the kitten yet, but we can sing her a lullaby."

We sang, ever so softly, ever so gently, as I settled her into her box.

Then, without any direction form me, the children wordlessly shared their understanding that they should move quietly toward recess. The universal sign for silence, a finger over the lips, passed from child to child. Heads nodded in agreement. Evan and Cathy tiptoed to the trashcan and back to their seats. Everyone took extra care in the closing of containers and lunch boxes. I smiled as the class moved in near silence toward their lockers.

This was a new kind of silence, not the silence that holds the dreamy wonder of first graders, but an alert, hushed moment of awe that arose from the livelier consciousness rooted in newfound cooperation of second and third grade children.

This is nice, I thought.

And so we entered a time of grace. It was as if the kitten had cast a magical spell upon the class, a spell that lifted them to their best selves. They were only seven and eight years old, but they were like the parents of a newborn baby, ever focused on their infant, ever forgetful of themselves.

Our life with Llyan, the name we gave the little kitten, evolved as she opened her eyes, became steady on her paws and began to explore her box and then our classroom. In time, children took turns carrying her box, dispensing kitten food, filling water dishes, holding her and stroking her increasingly fluffy, white fur.

Llyan called forth gentle hands and gentle voices, and a mood of caring. A new atmosphere of engaged wonder swept into our classroom like the soft fog that rolls landward from the bay. With the kitten in the room, everything was softer.

I continued to follow Steiner's advice to meditate on each child in the class. Every night I made an imaginary journey that began on the mainland, traveled across the bridge to Cape Cod, down the bay toward Falmouth, then headed east toward Hyannis. As I pictured each town, one by one, the faces of the children who lived there blossomed in my inner vision, often complete with an expression that I had seen that day, a grin, a frown, a look of wonder or surprise. My nightly meditation ended far away in Washington, D.C., where Marc and his family had a temporary residence for this school year. I imagined Marc with his trademark smile and, invariably, this image triggered a fond smile of my own.

I didn't expect that anything mysterious would come of my nightly musings, but I wasn't sure that nothing would come of this either.

And, I liked doing it. I liked seeing each face in my inner vision. I liked taking time, far from the bustle of the school day, to look at the class in silence. And, I liked the daily discipline of embracing what I felt to be the inner essence of each dear child.

It was a simple act of deliberate attention. Deepak Chopra said, "Love is attention without judgment." Was Steiner's prescription to teachers to engage in this ritual of attentive thinking his way of assuring that teachers would love their students? Was his wonder-centered curriculum a way to hold the attention of children so that they would come to feel love for humanity and for all that they learn?

Now, every evening, the sleeping kitten joined me in my dimly-lit living room as I visited briefly with each child, then turned on the lamp and opened my planning book, hoping that the magic of the meditation would somehow steer my plans for the next day toward the needs of each person in the class.

One day in November Llyan bounded across the classroom, ran up a row, then scooted under Reesa's desk.

"Llyan can run around the room while we eat," I had told them. "But we can't play with her, just quiet watching, no touching."

Llyan arched her back and rubbed against Rebecca's leg. Cathy, Megan, Evan, and Jamie echoed Rebecca's muffled giggle as Llyan tickled her way over their feet, between their legs and under their chairs.

Everyone laughed, but nobody laughed too loud. Everyone watched the kitten, but nobody reached down to pet her. Cautionary words, "Here she comes, don't move your feet," were offered in a friendly whisper. I beamed at my children and knew for a fact that I could, if I wished, walk out of the room and count on their continued restraint and their ongoing care for their little friend.

Later that afternoon Llyan rested in her box while the children molded colored beeswax. Then, the drum-like sounds of a big, burly kitten leaping against the cardboard sides of the box enlivened our lesson. Everyone giggled. Then it was quiet. "Look," said Jonah, "I can see her paws."

Llyan gripped the edge of the box, unable to pull herself over the top, but afraid to let go. I lifted her and placed her in the center of her nest, and said, laughing, "I think it is time for Llyan to find a new home."

The words were barely out of my mouth when the clamoring began.

"Can I have the kitten?"

"But I want the kitten."

"But, you already have a dog."

"I can ask my Mom if I can have a kitten."

"I already *know* my parents will let me have a kitten. They said we could get one."

My ill-considered statement was a sharp, cold wind that swept away the gentle fog. We suddenly returned to different reality. Only a moment ago my children had been soft, gentle, and caring. Now, the room felt cold and hard and the self-interest that had been shrouded in the blanket of mist became clearly visible again.

The magic was gone. The wonder was, again, missing. We had returned to a consciousness in which it made some sort of sense to argue about the ownership of a chewed-up pencil, the consciousness of easy misunderstandings, of me-first, of cold glances and selfish gestures.

I wanted to take back what I had said. I wished I had had the sense to figure out a plan for Llyan's future before mentioning anything to the class. But I hadn't, and now it was too late.

I foresaw that we would enter a time when our darling white ball of fluff would no longer cast a magic spell, but would, instead, spark divisiveness. I glanced ruefully at the closet where the eighth grade box rested on an upper shelf. Finding a home for Llyan was not going to be as easy as finding a place for a chewed up green pencil.

"I am going to have to think about this for a few days," I said.

We went back to our lesson, but the topic did not go away.

That day, and in the days that followed, children found moments before school and during recess to approach me individually to tell me that their parents would allow them to keep the kitten, to explain why their house would be better than a house with a dog or another cat, to tell me how their old cat had died and that they still had cat food and bowls and a nice little bed. Now an element of competition existed among us, that well-known motivation to be first, the best, to get the prize, in this case a white fuzz-ball of a kitten. A mood of competition cannot peacefully co-exist with a mood of wonder, for competition dispels a mood of awe as a hawk scatters a flock of doves.

One night I took the question of a home for Llyan into my meditation. I closed my eyes and waited for a mental picture of a new home, but no such image appeared.

I wonder if the expression, "it dawned on me," comes from the "ah-ha" experience that commonly arrives unbidden as the sun rises after sleeping on a problem. Rudolf Steiner suggested that such insightful realizations are born in conversation with spiritual beings and with each other during sleep.

Whatever the source of my insight, I rose the next morning to sunlight sparkling through the ice crystals on the skylight and a mental image of Marc, his face alight with his greatest grin, holding a fluffy, white kitten.

I was the only one who knew that this would be the last day that Llyan would scamper across the classroom before school. Arrangements for sending Llyan to Marc in Washington, D.C., had fallen into place quickly. Marc's Mom was in town for a short visit and she had happily agreed to transport Llyan in her car. The children knew none of this.

That morning I watched Jonah lift the robust kitten, hold her face near his and snuggle his nose into her soft fur. I remembered his silent, thoughtful reaction to losing the contested pencil to the eighth grade box. This time, though, the prize was far more dear than a chewed up pencil and everyone, not only Jonah and Reesa, felt entitled to be the winner. I braced myself for a room full of disappointed faces, for arguments and perhaps even tears.

It was the end of Main Lesson when I began my announcement. "I talked with Marc's Mom yesterday. She is back home for a visit. She is driving back tomorrow, so we have a chance to send Marc a Christmas present."

I paused, thinking about how to tell the class about my decision to give Marc the kitten, preparing myself for the inevitable disappointment, the quarreling.

But, in this moment of silence, Diana stood, her eyes wide open. A warm smile spread across her face as she felt the import of her idea before she spoke it. "The kitten," she shouted, "we could let him have Llyan."

Skipping the formality of raising his hand, Evan, Marc's closest friend, added excitedly, "And next year when he comes back he can bring her to school and we can all see her again."

"Can we, can we give Marc the kitten?" Jamie asked in a beseeching voice that was followed by a chorus of his pleading classmates.

"Can we?"

"Can we?"

I was both stunned and delighted. I had expected arguments and, instead, here was generosity.

I smiled broadly at the class and said. "I hoped that we could give Marc the kitten. So, I already asked his Mom if they would like to have her." I paused and smiled before continuing.

"She said yes."

The room exploded with happy smiles and many simultaneous, animated conversations.

I knew instantly that I had judged the class unfairly. The kitten had not, as I had imagined, brought a magical transformation to the class. Nor had my unplanned words dissipated a fragile selflessness engendered by this special little creature.

I had underestimated my children. Moments of selfishness might arise frequently in second grade. But these moments did not represent the essential nature of eight- and nine-year-old children any more than a misspelling or a mistake on a math problem. Llyan had not brought magic, she had simply given the class an opportunity to reveal the deep well of kindness that was at the core of their true selves, the capacity for reverence that flows readily when a mood of cooperation is maintained.

It was December and we were about to lose a classmate. She was tiny and cute and tended to interrupt lessons with loud bawling and banging on the walls. She had too much unrestrained energy to stay in the class. She would not sit in a chair. She distracted everyone. We didn't mind her antics, but we all knew it was time for her to move on. After all, she was a kitten. And our sadness in losing her would be overcome by our joy in knowing the happy smiles she would elicit from our dear, dear friend.

11

Work

In the ninth year the child really experiences a complete trans-
formation of its being, which indicates an important transfor-
mation of its soul-life and its bodily-physical experiences.
                                        —Rudolf Steiner

WHEN I WAS A CHILD my father owned a factory that put coatings
on paper, turning it into wrapping paper or the red paper with complex patterns used on a box of chocolates.

Block long, red brick factories were still the lifeblood of Pawtuck-
et, Rhode Island in those days. Even as young children we knew that
it all started with Samuel Slater, the colonial rebel who did not let
English law stand in his way. Exportation of plans for textile machin-
ery was prohibited in order to keep the colonies dependent on the
motherland for cloth. Sam worked in an English textile mill where
he memorized the shape, size, and function of every bolt, shaft, and
gear. He smuggled these invisible diagrams to the New World, hidden in his mind. Sam's textile mill, the first in America, still stands by
a pleasant waterfall across the Blackstone River in downtown Paw-
tucket. My Dad's factory sat on the other side of town in the middle
of a residential neighborhood.

My brothers and I had the run of the place on weekends while
our Dad built a boat in a corner of the quiet building. We sat at the
big double desk Dad shared with Grandpa, tried out the typewriters,
played hide and seek amid the dusty car-sized cylindrical boulders of
paper stacked in the warehouse. We peeked in the men's lockers and

peered into enormous vats of paints that emitted the pungent-sweet smell that permeated the machine room, the warehouse, and the office.

If I could take anything from my father's mill, it would be that smell. I would keep it in a bottle and open it while I prepared my lessons. And the aroma would waft over me and set a mood for work, for the toil that stands behind the gleaming gift. In this case, it was a gift invisible, the gift of a story that might contain a new math concept, a bit of history or a metaphoric map for the journey of life.

As I sat in my lesson factory, otherwise known as my living room, late at night, and early in the third and fourth grade year, I turned a story over and over in my mind. It was an old story, a familiar tale that I did not have to learn, only to dust off, polish a bit, and wrap in the shiny paper of a captivating introduction and vivid descriptions.

It wasn't my idea to tell the story of Adam and Eve in the third grade, to lay before my nine- and ten-year-olds this tale of temptation, of sin and banishment from paradise. This story was an ancient treasure I was expected to set before my students, not because of its religious content, but because it was one of those metaphorical maps.

If ever there was a time when a child needed a map it was at this age, at nine and ten years old. My kids had been drifting out of paradise since first grade. Magic, timeless comfort, and a sense of dreamy, floating oneness had been largely replaced in second grade by an ability to define and move step-by-step toward their own objectives. The new ability on the part of each child to move forthrightly toward his or her own goals had led to collisions with classmates on their own trajectories. Second grade had been a time of learning patience, of learning how to honor ones own intentions while still caring for the feelings of others. This change was part of an entire constellation of transformations in my students, big changes, happening day by day, week by week, month by month.

᭘

Burgeoning physical growth and ever new abilities of babies and toddlers make understanding much of their development a matter of
simple observation. One day the baby takes one step and then two.
School age children also move through milestones as profound as
learning to walk, yet, since so many of their transformations involve
their invisible, cognitive abilities and their overall consciousness, we
are often unaware when they reach a new threshold.

Parents and teachers often turn to developmental psychologists
and physicians to describe the inner first steps of the school age child.
Piaget, the father of developmental psychology, saw a significant shift
beginning at age six and seven, during the first grade year. While five-,
six-, and even seven-year-old children rely on fantasy to make sense
of their experiences, children who are eight and nine develop a new
understanding of the world based in reality. For instance, according
to Piaget, a younger child might have no trouble believing that a tall,
thin vase, containing only water poured into it from a full measuring
cup, now has more liquid than was held in the shorter, wider cup.

By the time that child is nine, however, he or she understands conservation of matter and, therefore, will see that, while the tall vase looks
like it holds more water, it must contain the same amount as the shorter, wider cup. This change in understanding is one small example of the
transformation that occurs during the first few years of grade school.

At all ages wonder arises when we cannot comprehend something marvelous that we see or hear. At first, as babies and young
children, we do not take the next step beyond awe, do not seek causes,
explanations; we just float. Young children come into a time when the
initial awe is magnified by a story they tell themselves or a story that
they are told. Now, in third and fourth grade, we had moved out of

an era when wonder tended to grow from imagination and we were about to cross a threshold into a time when the experience of wonder would, increasingly, be rooted in reality.

By third and fourth grade we had been through interpersonal disagreements and class-wide disputes. We had traveled far from the fairy tales of first grade and the unhurried approach to literacy favored by Waldorf schools for first graders.

The evolution from being a little kid to being a big kid had been going on for a long time for my students. But, like all children still in the shadow of the protected forest of paradise at age eight, they did not know they had stepped beyond the perimeter of that ancient grove. It was not until now, in third and fourth grade, that my students—like all children—would step beyond the shadow into the heat of the sun. It was not until now that they would, each according to their own inner timetable, come to an inner experience of this transformation from being a "little kid" to being a "big kid."

And, that inner experience would, in so many ways, be echoed in the story of the fall from grace, the banishment of Adam and Eve from paradise.

I thought about how it was a harsh story, though, so unlike the stories with happy endings that I told in first and second grade. Yet, it seemed to be especially made for my third and fourth graders who would each wake one day soon with the realization that something big had changed. They would search for the lost key to the fairyland of early childhood. Unable to go back, they would experience a previously unknown feeling of being separate from the world. Some would experience a deep sense of loneliness. Others might become emboldened by their new sense of disconnection and, like Rebecca's statement made with a puddle of water on a chair, they might experiment with actions of defiance. All of them would come to a daunting awareness that they now faced the almost-grown-up world of home-work, chores, deadlines, and consequences that would lead them day by day to the adult world of work.

I remembered my daughter, Nora, in her third grade year, sobbing, "I'm never going to be like Hannah again. It's so unfair. She's always laughing and fooling around, like a little kid." Hannah, the youngest child in her class, had short blonde, stick-out pigtails, an open smile that lived on the edge of a giggle, and a joyful exuberance that carried recess back into the classroom. Nora, the oldest child in her class, had tidy braids, a serious demeanor, her nose in a book and new spells of loneliness that could not be hugged away by mom. Nora had crossed the inner bridge into a realm of solitude and responsibility. I did not know how she knew it, but she could see that Hannah was not yet ready to cross that bridge, that she still lived in a land of innocence.

The next morning I tried to radiate that sense of innocence as I began telling the story. I thought of Hannah as I portrayed the wide-eyed wonder of Adam as God introduced him to creation. As I moved through the familiar scenes of the forbidden tree, the beguiling Satan, the first bite, the second bite, the discovery of nakedness and shame, the angry God, I felt the mood of the class grow deep and somber. Finally, with intensity in my voice, I acted the part of God and then the part of the wrathful angel. Cathy's eyes grew large as I raised my voice. Evan flinched as I raised my hand to banish the sinning couple. Then I told how Adam and Eve were forced from paradise to work by the sweat of their brows. And that was it.

A sea of faces stared at me in disbelief as sounds of children in the hallway searching through lockers confirmed that this was, in fact, the end of the lesson, that we were done for now, that we would eat our snack and go out to play and that, today, there would be no happy ending.

It was the next day that I looked forward to, the day when the children would tell me what they remembered of the story, when we would discuss their reaction to it.

I wasn't surprised when the class remembered each detail, when my tone of voice was imitated, when it was apparent that the shocked silence that followed the fall from grace into the realm of toil, still filled the room like the sweet-pungent odor that permeated the paper factory.

From the depth of that silence, Andy raised his hand. He was one of the oldest students in our combined class, a fourth grader. I nodded toward him. "You know what I think?" he asked provocatively. There was something urgent in his tone of voice that drew the class in. "I think it was good that Adam and Eve bit the apple." He paused.

I could almost hear his classmates asking through the shocked silence, "What do you mean Andy?"

"I mean, if they didn't bite the apple we wouldn't even be in school right now, we'd all be out there," he pointed out the window, "running around naked."

The room was silent for just long enough for this idea to sink in, then the class erupted. Rules about raising of hands and waiting to be called on were suspended by an instant, invisible, unanimous vote. Everyone spoke at once. Some children spoke directly to Andy, while others addressed their neighbors in confidential whispers, and a few raised their voices to try to speak to me.

I let the cauldron bubble for a few minutes and savored the intensity of the class's first passionate argument. Then I said, "If you agree with Andy that it was a good thing that Adam and Eve bit the apple, get up and walk over to the blackboard near the door. If you disagree with Andy, get up and walk over to the windows."

It was as if the discussion moved out of mouths and up into eyes and down into feet. The two camps slowly and silently divided into

Andy with his horde facing a group of only three girls. Megan, Cathy, and Rebecca did not agree that the fall from grace was a good thing.

I could see something in each of these girls, something of personality or life circumstance, that would cause them to cling to innocence. Yet, this insight did nothing to explain the tension I perceived between these two groups of children.

Entire sentences, paragraphs, perhaps encyclopedias, shot back and forth between the two groups in questioning glances, accusatory looks, defiant stares and apologetic postures.

And I, who was generally able to read the mood of the class, stepped back realizing that I had no idea what these two groups were saying to each other in this living silence. Theirs was an unspoken language of children, of nine- and ten-year-old children, and I was no longer privy to it.

Finally, Rebecca, the oldest of the three girls and clearly the expected spokesperson (even I knew that much) stepped forward. Her statement would show that she had a remarkable awareness of the inner change she, as a fourth grader, had already experienced.

"But," she began, in a tone that showed she was answering the accusing looks that faced her, "we wouldn't *know* we were naked."

12

Responsibility

In the beginning the child just plays, but he plays in earnest. There is only one dif-
ference between the play of the child and the work of the adult. It is that the adult
adapts himself to the outer utility that the world demands; his work is determined
from without. Play is determined from within, through the being of the child
which wants to unfold. It is the task of the school gradually to lead him over from
play to work. If we once find the answer to how we can metamorphose play into
work, we shall have solved the fundamental question of all early years education.
—Rudolf Steiner

THE CHILDREN AND I, with much help from their parents, built a
playhouse next to the sandbox. We designed it over the winter and
Philip's dad made architectural drawings that we copied into main
lesson books. Then, when spring came, small groups of students took
turns working with parent volunteers to erect the frame over a period
of a couple of weeks.

It was to be a real house, of wood and nails, sitting on cinder
block supports, with wide open window spaces on the south to let in
air and light and heavy pies passed in from the nearby sandbox. But it
was a symbolic house too.

The children did not know this of course, but I, like my cohorts
in Steiner schools around the world, chose the experience of designing and building a house as one of many ways of transforming the
experience of nakedness, loneliness, and vulnerability that comes with
being nine and ten years old. While the story of Adam and Eve was
meant to resonate with the children as they experienced their own fall

from grace, the building of the house was meant to be one of many ways to create a new connection with the world, a connection forged by work, by strength and by skill. Like Adam and Eve, the children would know work by the sweat of their brows and would rejoice in the fruit of their labor.

It was important that our measuring, sawing, hammering and pounding of nails would produce not just any carpentry project, but a shelter, a structure that would shield its occupants from the elements, would offer a sense of safety and protection, a feeling of being less naked, less exposed to the full heat of the sun. No house could return a nine or ten-year-old child to living in the sense of wholeness that predated their fall from grace. But, the experience of creating shelter could start an inner template, a rubric for the continual effort that would replace the innocent, effortless connection to the natural world and the people around them.

One shining spring day, the entire class, a few parents, and I nailed barn board siding to the wooden skeleton. I broke the children into teams and assigned each team a section. They had learned how to measure, hammer, and saw while working on the frame, so now it was possible to give them their tools, nails, and boards and set them to work with little adult direction.

The sounds of fourteen children sawing and banging reverberated through the school building. Faces of kindergarten children appeared at the windows. They watched in awe, as I once stood in awe of the work of the paper factory.

As the day grew warm, the skeleton became more and more enclosed. I smiled as my kids saw that the work of many weeks was almost complete and toiled without complaint in spite of the sweat on their brows.

Then, from the now invisible interior of the little house, I heard

Julia shout, "Ouch!" before she emerged crying and clutching her left arm.

"There's a nail sticking out in there and... and it, it scratched me," she managed to say between her sobs. I gave her a hug and inspected the scratch. It was a red scrape on the surface of her skin, with no bleeding. Rebecca and Megan stood close to their friend and I dispatched Rebecca to the office with Julia for washing, a band-aid, and a moment to calm down in the quiet of the building.

Megan disappeared back into the house. When she emerged Julia and Rebecca were already back from the office. Megan had made an important discovery and now she shared it with us: "The playhouse is *full* of sharp nails like that one. Sometimes the nails don't go into the frame like they're supposed to and they just stick out." Julia saw the problem, "Oh no! What if the little kids get cut like I did while they are playing in there?"

I stepped inside the house and saw that Megan was right. Here and there, a sharp point threatened to tear delicate skin. Ultimately, our little house would be a place of protection. But, at the moment, it was still a dangerous construction zone.

"Mrs. Allsup, what are you going to do?" asked Julia.

"I am going to appoint the three of you to be the building inspectors. We will not open this building to the rest of the school until you are completely satisfied with its safety. I'll show you how to remove or bend over the sticking out nails."

The three girls looked at me with shocked expressions. Julia said, "But it's not our fault."

We stood looking at each other for a moment.

I smiled at the three girls and handed each of them a hammer. "Sometimes we have to fix things that are not our fault," I said as an adult lifetime of such instances stirred in the back of my mind.

I would not have expected first or second graders to fix problems they had not created. I would not have expected such a level of responsibility then. But, now with my children nine and ten years old, I did. For, they were moving into a new phase. Something was turning, changing, awakening. I could see that they felt it too.

I didn't tell them that they would spend much of their adult lives fixing things that were not their fault. That they would wash dishes they did not eat from and laundry they did not stain. Nor did I tell them that they might someday choose careers that were, essentially, about fixing problems that they did not create. It can be satisfying, even wondrous, to right a wrong, to set things straight, to fix what has been broken, to be a force for order and goodness. I hoped that at a certain time in their teens or early twenties they would begin to eagerly seek out opportunities to be of service. But, for now, it would be enough to taste the satisfaction of working for the common good.

I was happy to witness the germination of that eagerness to help when Megan grinned and turned toward the house. "Make way for the building inspectors!" she shouted as she led her two friends into the building, hammers held high.

13

Inquiry

The outer world, with all its phenomena, is filled with divine splendor, but we must have experienced the divine within our-selves before we can hope to discover it in our environment.
—Rudolf Steiner

"TODAY, I want you to imagine the ceiling, the attic and the roof are missing and our classroom is open to the sun and the rain." I looked up as if I could see the clouds. The children did too.

"Now, imagine that you are a bird flying over the school and think about what our room would look like from way up there. What do you think a desk would look like?"

Hands shot up. "Evan, come up to the board and draw a desk the way a bird would see it."

Evan walked to the board and quickly sketched a desk that in-cluded legs. "Hm." I said, "I think you have drawn a bit more than the bird can really see. Think about this for a minute."

Evan squinted as he looked at his picture, took the eraser and removed the under parts of the desk.

"Good, that's close to what the bird sees." As Evan went back to his desk, I passed out paper.

"This will be your first sketch of the classroom from a bird's eye view."

Helen raised her hand. "Are you going to draw it on the board?'

"No, you're on your own this time."

I knew I was giving them a challenge and the finished drawings showed how difficult it is for third and fourth graders to create a map.

This was a fourth grade project in most Waldorf schools, but I modified the curriculum in my combined class and had moved to the curriculum of the older class by late winter. Now, at the end of our third and fourth grade year, we were well into fourth grade subject matter.

I held up each drawing and offered observations. "Look how Evan drew the desks large enough that they fill up the center section of the room. He didn't leave a lot of space between the desks and, when you look at our classroom, you see that there isn't a lot of space between the desks. That's realistic map making. Now look at Jamie's picture. He was able to figure out something pretty tricky. See how the blackboard in his picture is just a thick line. He doesn't show it as a rectangle because if the bird was exactly above it, the bird would not see the front of the board. It would only see the blackboard ledge that sticks out a few inches."

The next day I asked the students to make new drawings. These looked closer to the architectural ideal. Most of them were true to the bird's perspective and showed substantial desks rather than minuscule rectangles floating on a vast, white sea.

"Now you get to make a drawing at home," I told the class a few days later at the end of Main Lesson. "I want you to make one drawing for the first floor of your house and one drawing for the second floor if you have one. You should draw from a bird's eye view, the same way we drew the classroom."

Jonah raised his hand. "What if you live in two houses?"

"Then you can pick your Dad's house or your Mom's house, or, if you are really ambitious, you can do both."

Jonah picked his dad's house and the drawing he brought to school a week later had a special feature. I called Jonah to my desk to discuss his drawing.

"Jonah, what is this room in your dad's house?"

"I drew the kitchen and the living room and the bedrooms and the bathroom and then," he said shrugging, "there was just all this space left over in between."

"So you figure that in between these walls there is an area, sort of a room without doors or windows."

"Yeah, I guess so. I didn't know what to call it so... see," he pointed to an unintelligible scrawl at the edge of the area, "I just called it Nowhere Space."

"Nowhere space," I repeated, nodding and smiling. "I like that."

The next day I borrowed Nora's copy of *The Secret Staircase* by Jill Barklem. It is the story of a mouse family that finds a hidden staircase in the back of their tree house. This staircase leads to a maze of hidden rooms that all exist in what Jonah might call Nowhere Space.

"I have a book to read to you today," I told the class near the end of Main Lesson. "It's really a little kid's book, but it reminded me of something in Jonah's drawing of his dad's house."

I read the book to attentive, but not enraptured, listeners. After all, it was a little kid's book. Then I showed the class Jonah's picture and explained Nowhere Space. Jonah raised his hand and said in a matter of fact tone of voice, "I figured out that my drawing is messed up. I was at my Dad's house and I found out that I just drew it wrong, there really isn't a room in there."

"It's easy to do that when we draw buildings," I said. "But I still like the idea of Nowhere Space. It reminds me of a dream I had once. I dreamed I was in the house where I lived when I was your age. In the dream one of the kitchen cabinets led to a secret room over the garage."

As I said this, I looked at the clock near the door and noticed the time. "We can talk about this more later, but now we need to get our snacks."

We recited the short poem that marked the end of Main Lesson then some of the children walked to shelves in the back of the room to get lunch boxes. Others filed into the hallway to pull oversized backpacks out of their lockers. Those who remained in the room opened food containers and waited to begin our blessing. But Thomas, Jamie, and Marc did not return.

Instead, we heard their voices coming from the neighboring library. "Wow. I wonder's what's in there?"

"I think this really is Nowhere Space."

"Maybe it's part of the closet in the classroom."

Thomas darted into the room and opened the closet door. "No," he called out, the closet doesn't go that far."

Thomas, Marc, and Jamie now stood in the hallway just outside our room and stared at the door to our classroom and the door to the library. Logically, these two doors should have been no more than a foot apart. Instead, they were five feet apart and there was no accounting for what existed between the library wall and the classroom wall.

The buzz of excited conversation in the hall drew the rest of the class out of their seats to the threshold of our classroom. Their eyes were lit with a new sort of wonder, amazement at their own mysterious discovery, a discovery very much in the real world and not in their imaginations.

"It really *is* Nowhere Space!" said Jonah, appreciating this substantial space with no doors and windows that appeared to sit between our classroom, our closet, the library and the hallway.

"Mrs. Allsup, do you know what's in there?" asked Cathy. "Do you think it's a secret passageway?"

"I do have an idea what's in there, but I'm not going to tell you." I said raising my eyebrows as I motioned the class to their desks.

"Aw, come on!" complained Evan, "that's not fair."

"It's actually a pretty easy challenge," I said, smiling at him and then glancing at the area of the presumed Nowhere Space, taking care not to direct my eyes at the upper part of the wall. "Look carefully and you will figure it out."

We said our blessing. The children ate slowly, in silence, as they stared at the wall.

Then Philip tipped back in his chair and grinned. "Oh, I get it," he said. We shared a conspiratorial smile.

"Well?" demanded Helen.

"If Mrs. Allsup doesn't have to tell, then I don't either."

Then Jonah saw it too. "I see it. Just look up." he said, "Look at the top of the wall." All eyes looked at the three by five foot metal grille at the top of the wall that divided our room from the Nowhere Space.

"I get it," said Thomas, "it must be something to do with that air grate."

"Right," said Philip nodding his head and finally sharing his observation. "The air that goes into that grate has to go someplace. It must go down to the first floor and maybe even to the basement through that space."

"That must be why we hear noises over there sometimes." said Rebecca, "It's the air moving around."

"You're good detectives," I told them, "but it seems," I said, frowning and speaking in a slow and serious voice "that all your careful observation of that wall missed something over there that is really, really important."

"What?" asked Jamie as all faces turned to re-examine the wall and then turned back to me with quizzical expressions.

"The time!" I said laughing and pointing at the clock hanging on the no longer mysterious wall. "Don't you want to go to recess?"

The children laughed too. Then conversation turned to possible recess games as they packed up their food and poured into the hall.

Alone in the classroom, I walked to a window and gazed across the playground. Beyond the distant trees flowed the swift water of the Cape Cod Canal. I couldn't see the canal, but I could see the tall smokestack of a ship gliding behind the trees.

Usually, I did my best not to react to the daily parade of vessels as they moved behind the children's backs during our lessons, but now, in the empty room, I let my thoughts flow with the ship on the canal.

I was pleased that reading the *Secret Staircase* had helped to illustrate a concept. I had hoped that raising the issue of Nowhere Space would prod Jonah and others to think about their drawings of houses and whether, in fact, Nowhere Space was a feature of their homes. It had worked. Jonah saw his mistake without my telling him. And, the class began to look at our school building with a new spirit of inquiry.

But, just as I had felt a sense of chagrin at telling the harsh story of the Fall from Paradise, I now felt a sense of loss as I encouraged my class to explore the reality that stands behind the mystery.

I remembered the day I had been thrilled to share my discovery about a mysterious, invisible bit of spider's web. Then, my students were first and second graders. Then, I wanted them to dwell in a magical land where spiders' webs are held up by invisible forces, where fairies flit through the forest and where families of well-dressed mice might climb up a secret staircase in the Nowhere Space between the classroom and the library.

I supposed, if I found such a strand, today, with the class at the end of their third and fourth grade year, I would want my students to really examine the invisible parts. Now, I wanted my students to look carefully at all the invisible threads, at all the nowhere spaces, to ask questions, to try to see everything in their world, hidden and unhidden.

I liked our new, more mature form of wonder, but I remembered their little, round faces in first and second grade and allowed myself just a moment to notice my own sense of loss as they let go of explanations rooted in imagination and turned their older, leaner faces toward understanding the real world.

The sound of thunder in the stairwell stirred me from my reflections. I picked up a stack of main lesson books and carried them to the front of the room as children took their seats. "Helen, would you please pass out these main lesson books?"

I began my next sentence, "Open to…" but was not able to continue because Andy leaped from his seat, pointed toward the windows and called out, "Look!"

All heads turned to see what appeared to be the top of a large apartment building with huge smokestacks moving silently behind the trees. Then, without permission, the class rose from their seats as if this were the first ship that ever passed through the canal. They clustered along the window and gazed toward the passing container ship.

"Look at how big it is," said Marc.

Catherine said, "I think it's so big it's going to crash into the bridge."

"No it's not!" countered Helen.

Philip said, "I think that smokestack will come pretty close, but I don't think it will hit."

"Mrs. Allsup, can we watch to see if it hits the bridge?" asked Rebecca.

"Sure, we can watch," I said.

We waited. The ship did not crash into the bridge.

Before that day, no ship had ever been noticed by the children during a lesson and after that day no ship was ignored.

I don't know how they did it, for it is teachers, not students, who are known to have eyes in the backs of their heads. But, I assented happily to commercial breaks in my lessons as the children read the names of oil tankers, container ships, and barges taking the shortcut between Boston and New York. I was happy to pause in my lessons, because the children's amazed awareness of their world and all that moved through it was exactly what I wished for.

I often watched the children leaning on the window ledge as they gave silent, awed witness to the sight of what looked like majestic buildings gliding by. I listened to their comments on the features of the passing ships, the tall smokestacks, the pennants waving gaily from a topmast, the massive piles of colorful metal truck containers sliding behind the trees toward the Bourne Bridge.

And I was relieved to find that their transition out of innocence did not mean that they had lost their sense of wonder. For, now, with the cloak of early childhood torn away, they discovered the real world to be just as wondrous as the dream they woke from when they stepped out of Paradise.

14

Balance

We collect data, things, people, ideas, profound experiences, never pen-
etrating any of them ... But there are other times. There are times when
we stop. We sit still. We lose ourselves in a pile of leaves or its memory.
We listen and breezes from a whole other world begin to whisper.

—James Carroll

THE RACE WAS ON. Andy and Thomas sat poised, pencils gripped, eyes focused on the blackboard, ready for me to write an addition problem involving fractions. Quickly, I wrote a problem and smiled as I watched Andy drawing and writing furiously.

The rest of the class gathered around Andy and Thomas as they figured frantically. They inhaled as one, like a crowd watching an outfielder leaping toward a baseball flying toward the backboards. I was drawn into the drama of the race but, more than that, I was pleased to see my students passionately involved in their work, especially when that work was math. It is easy to help students find a soul connection to history or literature as these subjects are built of meaningful stories. But a deep and satisfying bond with mathematics can be harder to conjure.

I remembered that, as a child, I could remember complex methodologies for working with numbers if I understood the reasoning behind the number tricks. So, when I taught about adding fractions, I waited to show the short cut method and had the class use the painstaking method of changing the fractions so they had common denominators.

This approach stuck closely to the reasoning process, but it was cumbersome, so I introduced it with a story that offered a pictorial representation of the steps.

In the story, a French restaurant named "Maison de Quiche" was inhabited by a family of mice. The main mouse character was named Little Common Mouse, or LCM. The pictorial representation of the house, or "maison," and the journey of Little Common Mouse in it were designed to help the students remember the steps involved in using the Least Common Multiple (LCM) to add fractions.

Thomas learned the concept quickly and soon stopped drawing the picture of the "maison." This was typical of Thomas. In everything he tried to find the most efficient route. Most of the class, including Andy, held on to the imaginative way to add fractions. They carefully drew the little house each time. Sometimes they also added humorous drawings of the mouse, complete with a long curly tail, in their fraction house.

Thomas, in contrast, saw the little mouse as a bother from the start. The mouse and his silly house stood in the way of the pure concept, stood in the way of speedy calculation.

One day Andy noticed that Thomas had not drawn the house at all. "You forgot to draw the house," he said.

"I didn't forget," said Thomas, his eyes still on his work, "It's faster without it."

"It is not," countered Andy.

Now the whole class was listening.

Jonah said, "How about we have a race."

I was convinced from the start that Thomas, who had made the conceptual leap that allowed him to move into a more abstract understanding, would win easily. But I was wrong. Andy was a fast writer who executed drawings and calculations with impressive speed. Thomas, who had less to write, made his calculations in a more deliberate manner. The race was a dead tie.

One morning a few weeks after the fraction race, I took a deep breath and smiled at my students, bent over books, writing a composition about bobcats. Behind them a barge, pushed by a tugboat, lumbered up the canal. Our new classroom, across the hall from the room where we had explored Nowhere Space, featured an even better view of the canal and the bridge. But, this year my students did not turn around and rush to the windows. Now fourth and fifth graders, they worked with such concentration that an entire fleet of tall ships could have slipped by unseen.

As I enjoyed the productive silence, my thoughts drifted to a similar moment during our second and third grade year. One day in the spring of that year, while the class was drawing, I had found myself staring out toward the trees. I had been a teacher then for almost three years and until that moment I had never found myself free to look out the window during class time. My amazement had grown as nobody raised a hand. Nobody poked a neighbor. Nobody fell out of a chair. I had noticed the buds on the maple trees. I had noticed that I was noticing the buds on the maple trees. Maybe this will happen again, I thought.

This year, with my kids ten and eleven years old, I found a few moments in every main lesson to have my own thoughts.

Now, Reesa stood and walked toward me holding an open copybook. I had already circled places where punctuation should have appeared and underlined words with non-traditional spelling. I approved Reesa's revised version and then suggested she compose a few more sentences. Then I turned to Philip and then to Helen, who had come to stand by my desk, and held similar editorial conferences.

Helen returned to her seat and the room was silent again.

I stood, intending to wash the blackboard. But, remembering advice from a teacher in graduate school, I sat down again. "When the class is working, resist the temptation to get up and do something. Just sit for a while and watch your class. Enjoy them for a moment."

And so I did.

Reesa glanced up toward the clouds, then looked back to her paper again and again as if she were plucking ideas from the heavens the same way she once plucked falling maple leaves from the sky. Jonah leaned over and whispered to Marc, who offered him an eraser and a smile. It was the same smile that had flashed so often in first grade, yet not the same, just a bit guarded, just a bit deeper.

Thomas, bent over his book, gripped his pencil tightly, and wrote without a stray glance, his hand moving methodically across the page. I pictured Thomas in first grade, diving into his work after recess while his classmates chatted and waited for my directions. I remembered the fraction race and his insistence about dispensing with the superfluous mouse. Now, at ten years old, he had refined his ability to stay on task to an art form that wove each school day into a seamless tapestry of efficient work and well-organized play.

Thomas stood and stepped away from his desk. As he walked toward me I savored the depth of my connection to each of these children. Somehow it mattered that I knew them when they were little, that I could still see in each of them a first grade grin, a wild charge down the recess hill, a free and unconscious sociability not yet restrained by an understanding of classroom rules. Somehow it mattered that I had witnessed the big change from being little kids to being big kids.

It was important that in our moments of quiet concentration, while my big kids focused on their work, that I could still hear the raucous tumult of our first grade days, could still remember worrying that I could not meet the simultaneous needs of so many little people. Bit by bit, day by day, I had taught these children to not need me so much, to be increasingly independent, and yet they knew, and I knew, that in our newfound silence, I still stood by them.

Thomas placed his open main lesson book in my hands. I smiled. I knew exactly what he would say and exactly what I would say.

I began to review his completed composition about bobcats. I had not found anything to correct in his first draft in his copybook. Now I read this second version in his main lesson book, looking for spelling errors I knew I would not find, admiring the impeccable penmanship and the colorful border on each page.

"Nice job, Thomas." I said.

He thrust his hands into his pockets and uttered the expected five words, "Now what should I do?"

I thought, as usual, about the list of possible tasks that did not apply to Thomas, cleaning his desk, fixing errors in math homework, catching up on past assignments. I glanced again at his composition, looking for something that he might not have covered, something he could write about. But, he had covered all the points I had made in my presentation about the secretive feline that inhabited the forests on the mainland side of the canal.

I suppose, Thomas," I said, pausing for mock suspense, "that you could...." I paused again and raised my eyebrows, then finished with the usual words, "read a book."

"OK," he said, smiling and feigning surprise.

A novel already lay open on his desk.

We were in a month-long block about animals, and, in Friday's main lesson, I planned to tell the story of another mammal. During the summer I had written one animal name on each calendar day for this block. Now, as I wondered how to gently help Thomas seek and find moments of deep peace to punctuate his busy days, I found it appropriate that my plan called for me to present the quintessential overachiever of the animal world, the beaver.

Yet, as I smiled at my attentive students on Friday morning and began an unusually energetic presentation, I knew that the busy beaver was, in fact, the perfect animal to carry a message about balancing industrious work with contemplative rest.

For my commentary on the beaver in spring, summer, and fall, I spoke quickly and pitched short questions to the class. My gestures were swift and strong as I imitated a beaver hauling trees, swimming and gnawing at branches.

Then I slowed down and talked about the beaver in winter, resting in his warm lodge, feasting on his cached food. I breathed deeply, moved deliberately, and spoke of how animals and people both need to intersperse activity and rest.

The next day when I opened our review of the beaver, Thomas's hand shot up first. But I called on Evan and asked him to talk about beaver activity in the summer and the fall. Then I called on Rebecca to tell us about beaver lodges, Helen to review beaver dams, and Philip to explain the animal's fall practice of storing sticks underwater for his winter meals.

Next I asked the class to think of adjectives for the beaver in summer and fall. They poured out words in quick succession: busy, industrious, fast, hard-working, productive, active, energetic.

I knew that Marc could do justice to the beaver in winter. He had become a student who liked deep questions and who tended to intersperse his presentations to the class with long contemplative moments illuminated by a thoughtful smile. As he spoke, with slow, laconic sentences, it seemed that Marc would enjoy being a beaver in his winter lodge, safe from predators and the elements, with a cache of food nearby and the warmth of family about him. Listening to Marc, our breathing slowed and relaxed smiles appeared across the room.

"Now," I said, "it is time to think of adjectives for beaver in winter. Take your time and think of the best word to describe a beaver resting in his lodge. Let's just be quiet for a moment and wait for a word to come to each of us."

Philip stretched. Reesa looked out the window. Thomas leaned back in his chair, his eyes unfocused.

"I think we all have a word in mind, but I am going to only call on one person to share his adjective. Let's listen carefully to that one word."

"Thomas?" He raised his eyebrows as if to say, "but I didn't raise my hand."

Thomas rose and walked slowly to the front of the room. He stopped and took a slow, deep breath and then he said only one word, his eyes focused at a distant place, perhaps at a far away lodge where sleepy beavers snuggled together.

He took a deep breath and slowly uttered one word.

"Cozy."

His eyelids closed slowly and opened again and he took another deep breath. I shared a warm smile with the class. We all breathed more deeply as he walked slowly to his seat.

Years ago a professor had given me a simple image, that of a teacher sitting quietly for a few minutes enjoying the silence, enjoying the sight of her students working. He tossed us this image only once, but I had caught it and kept it with me. It was a small gift that had made a big difference in my life as a teacher. It had helped me to stop, to look back, to experience my own wonder at the miracle of transformation.

Thomas had caught the image of the restful beaver in winter. I hoped that he would keep it too. Yet I knew that the tendency toward strongly focused work and play lived deeply in Thomas. It would take more than this to lead him to the enjoyment of drawing little mice, to a slower and more relaxed approach to work, to an occasional moment for looking out the window at the drifting clouds.

I would one day send Thomas off to other schools and other teachers, still wishing that he would someday find his own way to the peace of the winter beaver.

I could not know this in our fourth and fifth grade year, but in seven years I would attend a high school graduation for four of my students. Here Philip would receive an award for his writing, Evan would receive an award for art, Marc would receive a spontaneous ovation, just for being his smiling, friendly self, and Thomas would deliver the main address. He would talk about how he began high school with a dedication to work that consumed almost every waking hour. Hundreds of people assembled in folding chairs on a great green lawn on a bright June day listened attentively as Thomas spoke eloquently about coming to an epiphany, about his realization that life is more than work, that he needed to sometimes close the books and look out into the sunshine.

Listening to Thomas, I smiled and then cried tears of joy. It had taken many years, but he had come to this epiphany on his own and now he was sharing is hard won insight with others. My wish for Thomas had been granted.

15

Insight

This concept of metamorphosis can, if desired, be applied to the whole of nature.
—Rudolf Steiner

"WHEN I WAS YOUR AGE I often went to the park to catch tadpoles."

I was nearing the conclusion of my presentation about frogs and I thought I would end on a personal, thoughtful note. I had talked about how tadpoles grow legs and absorb the tail and turn bit by bit into frogs. I had explained the big word, metamorphosis. Now I thought I would hint at a different but similar process of transformation, the metamorphosis we all experience in growing from childhood into adulthood.

"Hundreds of tadpoles lived in a shallow pond alongside the flower gardens. We caught them with a net then put them in a pail of water and looked at them. You could see the tiny legs just starting to grow. Later in the summer we caught the frogs they had become. We let these go free after watching them hopping in our pails. Sometimes they still had a bit of a tail.

"One day I was remembering how much fun I had catching frogs at the park and I told Mr. Allsup about it. He was quiet for a moment. Then he said, 'I used to catch frogs there too.'

"We both looked at each other thinking the same thing. We lived three miles apart when we were ten years old and we didn't know each other. We wouldn't be likely to see each other in our own neighborhoods, but we could have easily seen each other at the park that was halfway between our houses.

"We talked about how we both spent a lot of time at the park, es-pecially in the area with the garden and the ponds. The more we talked, the more likely we thought it was that we had seen each other there.

"We both thought it was strange to think that even though we met formally for the first time in high school, perhaps we met casu-ally, without learning each others' names when we were ten or eleven years old. Perhaps, unknowingly, I had shared a tadpole bucket with the boy who would become my husband.

"If you had told me then at the frog pond that the blond boy from the other side of the park would be my husband someday, I would not have believed it and I would not have understood the metamorphosis I would go through in the years ahead to come to that place where I wished to marry that boy. I would have been like a tadpole looking at a frog, unable to understand how she would one day be able to hop out of the water."

This was something to think about, a concept beyond the miracle of metamorphosis itself, the difficulty, the impossibility, of compre-hending the experiences that would come after we have made the next change and the change after that.

I knew that in putting this idea in front of fourth and fifth grad-ers, I was asking a lot. Rudolf Steiner recommended telling children things they would not understand. Sometimes, he said, these nuggets would surface later at a time when they would be of use. Would this idea be one of those nuggets saved for later, or would my class take this home now and ponder it, wonder what it will be like to be teen-agers, then to be in college, then to be married with a family? What would they take from my little story?

I looked at the clock and remembered my promise to supervise an early recess. There would be time to consider this later. We said our closing verse for main lesson. Some of the children went to their lockers to find their snacks. But Thomas, Philip, Jonah, Andy, Evan, and Marc, and a new classmate, Jeremy, all the boys in the fourth and fifth grade, except for the other new boy, Roland, skipped eating entirely and hurried to the recess waiting area at the top of the stairs. I poured a cup of tea from my thermos, took a few quick gulps, and, keeping my promise, joined them in the hallway. I nodded and they flew down the stairs.

One of the boys would duck into the gym for a basketball and they would be minutes into the game by the time the girls and I chatted our way down to the blacktop. And, more to the point, they would have time to play on their own before the sixth graders joined them.

Complaints about the sixth grade version of a basketball game had spiced our lunch conversations for weeks.

"They always break the rules. They just don't care."

"They don't even want to keep score."

"They're always fooling around."

It had been Thomas's idea to play ten minutes of fast, competitive basketball with rules while the older class still lingered over their pretzels. So, the girls and Roland and I had humored the basketball players' request by agreeing to a very quick snack.

Now, before the arrival of the older class, the game was silent and serious, choreographed by the incomparable grace of ten-year-old children who live in the innocent pause between being unskilled, little children and awkward adolescents. The six boys dribbled, swiveled, ran, blocked, leaped and shot the ball, according to the rules, while a group of girls played four square and a knot of fifth grade girls and Roland conversed beneath the trees.

Roland hung near the edge of the group of girls. Mostly, he listened. He was technically a fourth grader, but, because he had repeated a grade, he was as old as the fifth graders. And, since Jamie had left the class, we now had only one other boy his age, Andy, who was more likely to play basketball than to engage in conversation. In our small, multi-aged class, Roland appeared to occupy a developmental island all to himself.

The sixth graders bounced onto the blacktop. Boys and girls casually eased into the game in progress. They were good kids, every one of them, and I was anxious to observe the source of conflict between the two classes.

Suddenly, the game was no longer about dribbling and shooting. Instead, there was laughter, lots of semi-intentional body contact, jokes, more laughter, a girl falling over on purpose, the game stopping while the player is pulled to her feet by two boys.

It was clear this was never going to work. The fourth and fifth grade boys wanted, simply, to play basketball. The sixth graders, on the verge of adolescence, and living by a different understanding, wished instead for a social event under the guise of basketball. I made a mental note to ask my colleagues at the next faculty meeting to join me in figuring out a way to avoid a continuing collision of cultures on the basketball court.

Someday, my boys might care more about a girl's sweet smile than about how many times a ball popped through a hoop. But, for now, watching the flirtatious sixth grade antics was, for them, like tadpoles looking at frogs.

I had always enjoyed the part of main lesson called recall when the children told me what I had told them the day before. Now that my kids were old enough to analyze and discuss the issues raised in our lessons, I was especially eager to hear what they had to say.

Today I was looking forward to hearing not only about the life cycle of the frog, but also what they made of my personal story, their own ruminations about how difficult it is for a frog, or for a person, to understand his or her future condition.

Perhaps today would be the day that we reached a turning point in our journey. If the class was able to see how the tadpole views the world differently than a frog, see how a young person has a different experience than an older person, perhaps they were ready to understand lessons from history, to see how each culture created its own unique understanding of the human condition. A conversation about all of this led by the students themselves would be monumental, would show that we had rounded a corner, would signal a new phase of developmental readiness. I felt like a parent waiting for her child's first step, for that feeling of witnessing an opening into a new world.

And, like that parent, I also realized that it was possible that today would not be the day for such a transformation and that the ability to take that first step, like the ability to truly grasp certain ideas, could not be forced. It had to spring from a mysterious center of growth hidden within each child.

Perhaps, as I had speculated, awestruck contemplation about the evolution of human consciousness was far beyond their capacities at the beginning of their fourth and fifth grade year. As I opened the review of the lesson about frogs, I realized that perhaps they would have nothing to say about the deeper issues I had put before them. Pushing children to reach for something beyond their grasp can cause them to retreat or to leap awkwardly toward the impossible. It is the teacher's job to present developmentally appropriate lessons that can evolve into moments of wonder. But, even when the lesson is inspired and on target for the age range in the class, children cannot be led directly to wonder, nor can they be forced to find it.

We recapitulated the biology of frog development. Then I smiled at the class and asked, "Can anyone remember what I said at the end of the lesson yesterday, when I talked about my memories of catching frogs at your age?"

There was something in the room that said we were not ready for this discussion. My basketball players looked at me politely, but did not seem to register the question. I wondered whether they were thinking, "Couldn't we just stick with the frogs?" The fifth graders and Roland appeared only slightly more interested. Helen raised her hand.

Years ago, in first grade, Helen had shared her awareness of the never-ending continuity of the universe. Her vision had opened a door to an unexpected conversation, had lifted the class and me to moments of awe. During the four years that had transpired since then, I had come to count on her ability to delve into the essence of our lessons, to lead the class into deep conversations. Perhaps, I thought, this will happen again.

I nodded at Helen. In a moment she would speak. She would not say much, but she would say it all, summarizing both what I had said and the perspective of a ten-year-old on the topic of marriage. Her incisive recapitulation would be delivered with a finality that suggested that we postpone any deep discussions, that we would not be taking any first steps today.

Her voice was not soft and dreamy as it had been in first grade, but, rather, clear, strong, and decisive with no hint of the humor that she would deliver in the one liner that would bring our recall session to an uproarious close.

"Mrs. Allsup," she said, "You told us that getting married is like turning into a frog."

16

Hope

In all things it is better to hope than to despair.
—Johann Wolfgang von Goethe

UNFORTUNATELY, living a childhood that is rich in wonder does not guarantee a future that is entirely wonderful.

It is snowing lightly and it is dark and I am driving, driving with Nora, now fourteen, driving around town, driving along the shore, driving by our favorite Christmas lights that are strung through and through on every branch of a fifty-foot pine that shimmers in the wind like a flickering flame.

It is all about distraction, distraction from the relentless pain of the chronic migraine headaches that have redefined Nora's young life. We drive and we talk. She should be asleep. I should be sitting on the sofa reading and re-reading multiple versions of an ancient Norse legend, preparing, word by word, sentence by sentence, to tell the story the next morning.

I should be meditating on what it means to be a fourth grader, a student just beyond the nine-year-change, meditating on my students who seem twice as big as last year, a thundering herd who remind me of charging buffaloes, of the majestic Norse gods themselves. I should be learning the tricky Norse names. I should be figuring out how to-morrow's story will again foreshadow the catastrophic Ragnorok, the Twilight of the Gods, the shattering transformation of the ancient world of the Northmen. Instead, unbelievably, driving through the

December night, we are experiencing the foreshadowing of our own Ragnorok.

Nora doesn't go to school with me anymore. She doesn't go to school at all. The pounding headaches with visual disturbances that burst into our lives during her last year at the Waldorf School, exploded in her first months of high school. She became disabled by the frequency of these migraine headaches and could not keep up with the required pace of work. Now she is a home-schooler. Geoff and I phone her throughout the day and take turns coming home to check on her. If it is a day with a migraine, we find her asleep in her dark room. It is like death in life, a day that does not exist for her. If it is a good day, we find her with her little dog, Picabo, and her books, cheerfully pursuing a home study course.

We are now beyond the concern that the pain might be caused by a brain tumor. We know this is not a life threatening condition. I have read my way through a pile of books about this disease that is defined by headaches, but is more than headaches, a whole-body illness with nausea, and days of exhaustion with a level of pain that can be equivalent to the agony of breaking a bone.

Our local doctors have not been able to reduce the frequency of headaches. And the medicine they prescribe to ease pain makes Nora too tired and spacey to attend school. Even worse, taking the medication seems to trigger more headaches. So she has decided to avoid the drugs. We await an appointment at Children's Hospital in Boston. For now, the only cure seems to be sleep. A night of sleep brings relief in the morning.

Many nights, the pain is too much in the early evening and Nora can't sleep until late. She wants distraction from the pain, so we go out into the mystery of the night, to the stars, to the remembered wonder of a world brightened for Christmas. As I drive I tell her the stories I have been telling in class, the stories she knows from fourth grade about the Norse gods—Thor, Odin, Loki, and Iduna. We remember her role as Iduna, the bearer of eternal youth, in her fourth grade play. She mentions the long pink dress that still hangs in her closet and the basket of plastic, spray-painted golden apples. The gods in the story have to eat one of these apples each day in order to keep their youth. We wish for the medical equivalent of the magical apples and talk hopefully about her January appointment in Boston.

Mostly, though, we try not to talk about her medical condition. We get home by eleven and hang out together for awhile. At midnight, when Nora is finally asleep, I gather my books and learn the next story in the Norse saga. I am so anxious that I am able to stay awake until I have learned the essence of the story and have scribbled notes to remind me of the long Nordic names. I will get to sleep by one thirty and be up by six. My first thought upon rising is, "Will Nora have a headache today?"

I begin many mornings standing by Nora's bed, wondering whether I should stay home from school to care for her.

"Go, Mom," she says, "You really can't help me by being here and your class needs you. I'm going back to sleep. Yeah, it's a bad one, but I'm going to be OK."

So, I don't miss school. I go.

I manage to smile in class, to remember my old self and impersonate her. But, I am not wholly here. Nora is six miles away and I am with her in my minds eye. I stand at once before the class and by her bed, watching over her, blessing her, supporting her with all the inner strength I can muster.

Between classes, other teachers notice that I look tired and miserable. I seek advice from a colleague who has been through her own challenges with her child. Her wisdom is simple, but deep. "Sometimes," she tells me, "we just have to learn to live with sadness."

At a faculty meeting, I tell my colleagues about our long nights, about my worries, about getting four hours of sleep. A colleague suggests the unthinkable. "You have to get more sleep," he says. "Of course, it is our ideal to memorize the stories. But, for now, you are going to have to make an exception. If you read the stories to the class you can get a bit more sleep."

It is December of fourth and fifth grade and, for the first time ever, I come to school carrying a book, a canned meal, rather than a story known by heart, a lesson I have cooked up myself. The children ask why I am reading the stories instead of telling them from memory. I explain that Nora has been sick with headaches and that I am spending most of my evenings taking care of her. I apologize for being unable to learn the stories. Many of my students have known Nora since they were toddlers. I see concern on their faces. I tell them we hope the doctors in Boston will be able to help.

The stories are dramatic and I do what I can to bring the readings to life. My lessons are like canned stew, prepared elsewhere and preserved in a book. The class listens and is engaged, but it is not the same. Canned stew is never as delicious as the stew you cook yourself with fresh carrots, potatoes, and secret spices.

Then it is winter break. Anticipating that the weeks following vacation will give little opportunity for learning stories, I read and re-read the final chapters from my books on Norse Mythology. And, when I find myself with Nora, doing the late evening tour of Christmas lights, I practice by telling her the stories as we drive into the icy night.

"It was a winter far colder than any we have ever seen, when howling storms followed one upon the last and snow and ice piles grew into mountains and the rivers and seas froze and darkness fell.

"And then it was as if all bad things were let loose. Loki broke his chains and Fenris the wolf with his wide jaws and great teeth broke loose and the Midgard serpent emerged from the deep.

"Now the enemies of the gods gathered on the plain of Vigrid."

"It's strange," Nora said, "but I don't remember this part of Norse mythology. I think I must have had the flu or something the week my teacher told it."

It was an intense story, even stronger than the story of the fall from paradise that I had told in third grade, the story that had mirrored the children's experience of the nine-year-change. Now, the youngest children in my class were turning ten. They were half-way between kindergarten and high school. If third grade was about letting go of early childhood, this year was about tearing apart and recreating their inner reality, about laying a foundation for who they would be at fourteen. It was about less play and more work, about being serious students, about grammar, homework, fractions and long division. And it was readiness for a story that elicits a mature, adult form of wonder, the awe we feel when we witness rebirth after a time of desolation.

Long ago, Nora had gone through the transformation that had destroyed the magical inner kingdom of early childhood. In its place, she had laid a foundation for the high school student we all imagined she would someday be, an artsy, bookish, high-achieving student in a competitive high school environment replete with friends and congenial teachers. But the foundation she had built was for a house that would not be. The headaches had ripped apart this image of her teenage years.

So now it seemed strangely right that I should tell her the story of the Ragnarok, a story that calls up the feelings of desolation that come at a time of transformation, a story that shows that others have faced worse, much worse.

It also seemed right to invite Nora to come to school with me on that February day when I would tell the story of the rebirth that followed the Ragnarok. And so it was that on the morning when I told the story of the dawning of a new world, Nora sat in the back of my classroom and listened with my fourth graders.

It seemed that Nora too was at the brink of a new beginning. The Boston specialists had referred her to a practitioner of biofeedback. She practiced this religiously, and, by mid February, the headaches came less frequently. She was back in school, this time as an under-age student at Cape Cod Community College, which had accepted her as a part-time evening student. The two-hour classes were not as long as a seven hour school day, so sometimes she was able to attend even when she had a headache. Geoff and I took turns driving her to class; on my nights to drive, I learned stories and prepared lessons in the college library.

Nora's headaches did not go away entirely, but they became infrequent enough that she was able to develop a robust program that combined the evening college classes with daytime guitar lessons, voice lessons, a tightly-knit girls' social group, and lots of reading and writing.

In particular, she devoted herself to composing songs. Our house was silent on headache days, but now the healthy days grew in number, and on these days Nora's strong soprano voice, accompanied by rich guitar chords, reverberated through our little house with messages of hope, courage, and new life.

🌱

Childhood is the foundation for life, the anchoring structure that holds up the many floors of the unique house that we build in adolescence and adulthood. At fourteen, just stepping out of childhood into her teenage years, Nora was already experiencing a test of that childhood foundation.

The biblical parable says the house built to endure storms is anchored to a rock rather than sand. Most discussions about the future of elementary education assume that academic achievement is the rock-strong foundation for a child's future. Certainly, it would be wrong to doubt the importance of reading, writing, and math. As a parent watching Nora dive into adult level reading as part of her home studies, I was grateful that she had developed these capacities in grade school.

However, in the face of the storms of life, these capabilities are not what will necessarily endure, and competence alone is not what helps us to carry on. Like all Waldorf students, a key element of Nora's foundation rock was the habit of wonder. And, while her bad days continued to be very bad, she, somehow, had the wherewithal to make her good days really good.

Freud said, "Love and work are the cornerstones of our humanness." Wonder is the door to both of these. It is that living glimmer of openness, interest, and eagerness that causes us to notice that which is delightful, causes the heart to reach to another, ignites the will in working toward a goal.

We pray that children will experience few hardships, but the storms of life, poor health, dashed expectations, tragic accidents, and reversals of fortune come in some unpredictable measure to each of us. The habit of wonder, as Rachel Carson says is *"an unfailing antidote to...the disenchantments of later years."* After a trial, the habit of wonder brings us back to balance.

For Nora, the habit of wonder had to be deeply ingrained, strong enough to kick start her motivation to learn, to read, to write, to paint, to compose, to sing after each lost day.

For a time it seemed as if a new day had arrived. But, in truth, our Ragnarok was still to come. The challenges we had met so far had been but a foreshadowing.

But now, with Nora looking increasingly healthy and rebuilding an active life, I put my anxiety behind me and, again, found joy in my daily challenges.

It was a time of hope.

17

Friendship

Love starts when we push aside our ego and make room for someone else.
—Rudolf Steiner

OUR FIELD TRIP to the ice skating rink was a week away, but in my mind's eye, I could already see it. My basketball boys and most of the girls would circle the rink, skating smoothly, stealing gloves and chasing after the good-natured thieves. The girls would move to the center of the ice to practice twirls, spins, and lunges. Rebecca, an accomplished skater who took lessons, would, no doubt, grace this center space for the entire hour, skating in tight circles, backwards then forward, pirouetting, leaping, practicing a long choreographed routine that she was learning for a performance.

Roland had told me that he'd never worn ice skates. I imagined him looking like any new skater, clinging to the boards, creeping forward inch by inch, his ankles bent at weird angles, crashing and re-covering and crashing again.

I saw myself skating with him. It would not be as much fun for him to skate with a teacher as with a friend, but Roland still did not have a friend in the class.

New students at any school sometimes endure a lonely time of days, weeks, or months while they tread the mysterious path toward new friendship. Now, in late November, Roland appeared no closer to finding a soul mate than he had been the first day he joined the class.

Before school and at lunch and snack, Roland conversed only

with me. At recess he drifted around a circle of girls who did little to recognize his presence.

He was, by far, the largest student in the class, almost as tall as I. His broad shoulders and rugged, heavy-set frame gave him the appearance of a future football player. Yet, even though he looked like a fullback, I could not imagine Roland wanting to join any sort of athletic team.

I could picture the type of boy who would be an ideal friend for Roland. He would be a fifth grader who was a bit shy, who was more drawn to reading or board games than athletics, who would ignore the ever-present game of basketball and be happy to talk at recess while walking around the perimeter of the field.

That boy was not in our class.

In the absence of such a friend, Roland often chatted with me about his hometown, the animals at the local zoo, about traveling with his Mom.

We did not talk, however, about what had happened before he came to our school. I knew of course. His mother had told me about how his father had died unexpectedly while Roland was in first grade. Grandpa did the best he could to become the man in Roland's life. Then, within a year, he died too.

Everything became difficult. School became difficult. Roland repeated a grade and thus lost daily contact with his cohort of friends.

Eventually, Roland's devoted mother saw a new school as a place to start over. Our combined fourth and fifth grade seemed ideal for a fourth grader who was old for his class.

With the possibility of a long-term relationship with one teacher, a relaxed classroom environment with minimal testing and little time pressure, hours of painting, drawing, and knitting, a small class in a small school where everyone knew each other, we had the ingredients for a nurturing environment. We might even give Roland a healing environment, except for one thing, the crucial, necessary element—a likely candidate for friendship.

I had never been so frustrated as a teacher. Never had a child joined our class who so urgently needed a friend. Never had a child joined our class who was so unlikely to find one. I desperately wanted to make something right for Roland.

My imagination of the ice skating party had not included so much skate tying. Bent in half, I tugged at lace after lace, shaking my head at my expectation that fourth graders would be more independent.

Most of the children were finally on the ice while I held Reesa's left foot then right foot between my knees and pulled at the laces. Cathy was last, and then I donned my own skates and finally stepped onto the ice.

Across the rink I saw Philip in pursuit of Andy, both of them slaloming between their classmates, Andy holding Philip's red glove high in the air. Reesa and Cathy at center ice took turns attempting to skate backwards. I scanned this area for Rebecca, but I didn't see her. I searched the moving clusters of skaters, but I did not find Rebecca. Perhaps she is in the bathroom, I thought. Skating toward one of the parent chaperones I planned to ask whether she had left the ice.

Then I saw her. Rebecca stood at the edge with Roland. He leaned forward, gripping the boards, his ankles wobbling to and fro. Rebecca slowly skated backwards. Roland didn't budge. She skated toward him, turned, and demonstrated a short glide. Then she turned and faced him. Roland shuffled forward. From the other side of the rink, I could not hear them, but I could see that Rebecca was laughing, laughing in a friendly way, an encouraging way.

It was a comical sight. Rebecca was one of the oldest in the class, but still one of the smallest. A graceful pixie, she flew around a staggering giant who, bit by bit, became steadier on his skates and began to join in her laughter.

Circling the rink, I often glanced at Roland and Rebecca. Surely, I thought, she will leave him once he is stable on his feet. She will sweep into the center and show her stuff. Then it will be my turn to creep around the boards with Roland.

But, half way through the hour, when I told Rebecca I would be happy to take a turn as skating coach, she turned me down, saying, "No, that's OK, I'm having fun."

It was then that I realized that something more might be happening here, something more than a skating lesson. Perhaps it was Roland's vulnerability, his clear need for help that had drawn Rebecca in. Now, as I saw them clowning, saw other children stopping to visit with them and joining in the laughing and coaching, I could see that it was Roland's happy companionship that had caused her to stay with him even though I had offered her a reprieve from the duty of giving skating lessons.

Round and round I skated with my class, with joy evermore swelling in my heart as it became increasingly clear that today Rebecca would generously and happily sacrifice her leaps and pirouettes to skate with Roland for the entire hour.

I was a competent but cumbersome skater. But on that day, I flew effortlessly, lifted by my sense of happy amazement, by invisible wings on wind generated by newfound friendship, a fresh wind that would herald a sea change in the social dynamic of the class.

Back at school, Rebecca drew Roland into her circle of friends. It had not occurred to me that Roland did, in fact, have likely candidates for friendship and that they were the knot of students who were uninterested in basketball, the group that just happened to be composed, until now, of girls.

It was a breakthrough for Roland and it was a breakthrough for the girls too.

A sense of belonging helps develop the security that allows a child to invest energy in deep engagement in new concepts or knowledge. If one were to make a list of aspects of classroom life that are to some degree beyond the control of both teachers and parents, friendship would be near the top. In the sometimes precarious journey of a child, classmates hold an often unrecognized power.

Years ago, when we were in first and second grade, I had learned that it was not solely up to me to meet the needs of my students. I witnessed my kids unwittingly, beyond their intentions or understanding, taking care of each other. Now it was my turn to experience wonder as I witnessed my students purposely taking care of each other.

Rebecca had intentionally sacrificed an hour of her own enjoyment as a proficient skater to help a classmate and, in doing so, both had discovered doors opening to friendship.

Never had a child come to our class with such a desperate need for healing companionship. Never had I been so delighted to see a child find a comfortable berth in the social vessel of the class.

18

Freedom

The world will never starve for want of wonders; but only for want of wonder.
—G.K. Chesterton

"IMAGINE that you are crossing the Great Plains with your Conestoga wagon. Most days you do not ride. You walk alongside your wagon and the big sky arches over you and the prairie seems to go on forever, the rolling waves of grass like the endless ocean. The days are relatively easy now, but you know that challenges lie ahead, that you have to cross the mountains to get to the land where you will make your fortune, where you will dig gold nuggets from the hills. Your wagon is part of a long wagon train. Some of the travelers have painted big signs on the sides of their wagons. They say 'California or Bust' or 'Jones Family from Ohio.'"

It is mid-winter of our fourth and fifth grade year, and the class settles into listening, to a mood of expectation.

"Far off in the distance you see something moving though the tall grass. At first it appears to be a very large animal. Then you realize it is a covered wagon like your own. It is coming toward you heading east, going the wrong way.

"Everyone on the wagon train is filled with curiosity. Closer, closer it comes. As the wagon nears, you see a painting of an elephant and big letters on the dust-covered canvas that say, 'We saw the elephant.'

"Your children read the sign and see the big painting of an elephant that fills the canvas and they don't know what this means, so you tell them what you have heard:

"'Once a circus traveled through the countryside, often marching into a town with the elephant at the front of the parade. One day, a farmer riding horseback came around a corner and almost collided with the elephant. His horse sized up the beast as the scariest looking horse he had ever seen. The horse reared up, dumped his rider, turned tail and galloped all the way back to the barn. The farmer said, 'At least I've seen the elephant.'

"So when someone says that they have 'seen the elephant,' it means that they saw something amazing, or something scary and amazing, perhaps so scary that they turned around and ran away from it.

"As the wagon passes you wave and wonder whether these folks have encountered a deadly rattlesnake or a tornado or a river too deep or a desert too wide. You wish you could stop and find out whether they had found gold or whether they had been overwhelmed and turned around before they ever put a pan in a river or a shovel in the earth. You realize you will never know what the elephant means to them.

"The greatness of the sky and the openness of the prairie fill your heart with a new sense of freedom. And yet, as your vision takes in wagon after wagon moving west across the grassy sea, moving separately yet together, you find a sense of security in not being alone, in being part of a moving community of travelers."

I notice Roland as I deliver this part of the lesson, and feel grateful that he, like the pioneers in their wagons, has become increasingly secure in our community.

Ice covered, slippery snow has a grip on the blacktop and the field. I hope that our study of United States geography, especially the imagined expansiveness of the western skies, provides a balance to the confined feeling that comes with recess in the gym. I hope too that the adventurous spirit of the journey west is a metaphor that goes deep and becomes part of their rubric for a life of continual discovery. This lesson is a story within a story. The gold rush story is a segue from an ongoing series of lessons based on the non-fiction book by John Siegel Boettner, *Hey Mom Can I Ride My Bike Across America?* in which five students and their teachers bicycle from Maryland to California. On most days I retell accounts from the book and weave in factual information about the region they encounter in the episode.

Evenings find me on the sofa with Boettner's book, and a heap of library books—histories, travelogues, picture books about Illinois, Kansas, South Dakota, the Badlands, and the Grand Tetons. If it is an evening when Nora is not in class at the community college and she does not have a migraine, she sits nearby studying a book about Chinese history. When we take a break from our studies, our conversation often turns to the differences between Waldorf schools and other schools.

"My teachers in high school were good people and I liked them, but they didn't do what I see you doing tonight or what Mr. Rosen used to do. Did you ever see the piles of books that he got from the Harvard Library? I knew what he taught came from all those books and more. My history teacher in high school brought in one textbook. He didn't make a presentation or anything, just expected you to read it yourself. Then we went over what we read. Sometimes kids came up with their own ideas and sometimes the teacher said something that wasn't in the book. But lots of days, I didn't know why we even had a class. I mean, I can read. If a teacher isn't going to tell me something that is not in the textbook, not going to get us into a conversation where we have to think, I had to wonder, why am I there? Except for the fact that I am the youngest person in the room, and the subjects are more complex, the college courses I am taking now are more like what I was used to in grade school."

Nora's observations and my memories of the autumn weeks when I read my lessons from a book, rather than delivering them from memory, led me to feel more than ever that it makes a difference that I create my own lessons and that my students interpret them independently without the aid of a text book. Independent effort is an endangered pursuit in our culture.

We live with the widespread belief that passive experience can be as satisfying as active engagement, that the frozen pre-made dinner, the standards-based lesson partnered with a text book, the television programs and video games that occupy whole evenings, truly meet our needs for nutrition, education, and entertainment. But, in my mind, watching a climber reach the top of Mount Everest on television is less moving than a hike through the Four Ponds Conservation Area where a spider's web might be discovered hanging mysteriously in mid-air.

I survey my heap of books and it feels important that my creation of each lesson begins with my independent journey of discovery in which I am not obliged to use only one required textbook. Instead, I have the freedom to explore many sources, take what seems interesting to me and relevant to the class and weave it all together into my own special creation crafted especially for my class. It matters too that I expect that my students likewise will process what I have given them independently without a textbook or workbook, that their conversations, writing, and artwork about the lesson will all bear the stamp of their originality.

It is as if my class and I are pioneers on our own wagon train, heading west before the land was mapped, when each day would bring something unexpected and wondrous. For education works best when teachers are metaphoric leaders of a wagon train, not conductors on a train pulled by a locomotive. We build capacities in ourselves and our students when we each have to scout out our own way, when each student is a self-propelled traveler, when each wagon is free to stop, move slowly, to choose a personal course that avoids dust and ditches yet is still part of a community moving not on fixed rails but in a general direction connected by the invisible bonds of agreement and intention.

Sitting in our living and dining area, where we eat home cooked meals together each evening and rarely turn on the television, I think, too, about the increasingly predictable lives of children as far off strangers dictate the details of children's daily experience. Canned text book chapters, standards-based lessons, TV shows, and fast food meals lead children in Arizona, Kansas, and Maryland to all sing the same advertising ditties, answer the same questions for homework, and taste the same salty, greasy food from chain restaurants.

A standardized, homogenized, predictable life, structured by far off curriculum designers, food managers, and TV directors decreases opportunities to develop new abilities and chances for discovery. A child who pulls carrots and leeks from a home garden and helps to chop these, experiences amazement as as she pulls them from the soil, and finds satisfaction in a new ability to safely wield a knife and in sharing the meal she helped to create. A student who practices playing a flute for half an hour after dinner develops self-confidence as skills improve, sensory pleasure while hearing a beautiful melody and, eventually, satisfaction from sharing the music with others.

Our culture is starved for wonder. Yet, somehow we have become confused about how to find the experience of awed discovery. A sense of dissatisfaction could lead us to independent, creative effort, but instead, often leads to attempts to increase the number of passive experiences. Our yearning for the experience of awed discovery ironically propels us to quicken all things, to move through the world in speeding cars, bullet trains, and supersonic planes. Some think that learning, too, can be accelerated and that there is an advantage to covering more territory in less time.

My students will each write their own compositions based on what they have learned. They will remember our lessons well for the same reason the westward travelers remembered their journey and for the same reason I remember our bicycle-powered vacations better then our travels by car—because they expended personal effort each step of the way.

The same is true for a child's free time after school. Parents can support a version of childhood that builds capable adults by turning off the television and video games, providing their children with art supplies, musical instruments and lessons, and unstructured time in a forest or on a beach. Instead of video games, they could provide library books, bicycles, jump ropes, and sports equipment. Children who put real effort into their free time develop not only new capacities but also a sense of satisfaction borne of their own surprised amazement at their own accomplishments.

Teachers can strive to bring original lessons and parents can show their own pursuit of independent thought and action. Without ever speaking about these matters, it is vital to demonstrate that we have the power to shape our days, we have the will to learn and to work, that it is natural to find meaning in our work, and that we can respond in freedom to what comes our way.

19

Experience

You tell me, I forget. You teach me, I remember. You involve me, I learn."
—Benjamin Franklin

I HADN'T PLANNED to be barreling down the stairs at 9:30 in the morning with my fourth and fifth graders, demolishing the peace of main lesson for nearby classes. But I also hadn't expected that my class would not be able to answer what I thought was a simple question: "Why can't a river the size of the Mississippi River be on Cape Cod, on this side of the canal?"

Theories poured like a rushing stream and I smiled at each, then shook my head.

"The ground is too sandy and the water would just sink in."

"Cape Cod is not as wide as the Mississippi River."

"We don't have a lake that is big enough. Rivers start in lakes and a big river has to start in a big lake."

"We don't have any mountains and rivers start in mountains."

It seemed ironic that, here, in a region defined by water, my class lacked a basic understanding about the substance that played such a leading role in their lives. Cut off from the mainland by the canal, Cape Cod is surrounded by water. Since the digging of this waterway in 1914, our peninsula had essentially become an island, an island indented by the bays and estuaries that offered my students expansive vistas, summers of sailing and fishing, and days at the beach, swimming and working with sand, mud, and water in ways that might reveal the essential qualities of this element.

Yet, while fingers of the world's oceans tickled the banks of the canal a few blocks from our door, we were fresh water poor. Our measly fresh water supply flowed slowly beneath the ground, lay still in kettle hole ponds, and trickled in small streams that emptied quickly into bays. Like people who live on any small island, we did not have much personal experience with rivers. Many in my class had never seen a huge, muscular, mile-wide river. Waterfalls, dams, levies, and the rushing sort of clear water stream that splashes over rocks, all this was foreign to the students who now arranged themselves around the perimeter of the big sandbox.

Rudolf Steiner once said that ten hours of preparation should stand behind each hour of teaching. During teacher training, my classmates and I had laughed at the impossibility of this. How could we find 300 hours of preparation each week to precede the 30 hours we would spend instructing children? A wise professor had given us the answer: previous life experience.

It had taken me a minute to conjure up a plan for this outdoor demonstration. But, I had prepared for it over a seventeen year career as an environmentalist. Long before I had become a teacher of children, I had educated adults about rainfall, groundwater, street runoff, inland rivers, estuaries, shellfish beds, and bays so that they could help make informed decisions about sewage treatment plants, septic systems, and housing densities. Like many Waldorf teachers, I had been drawn into teaching out of another career.

I knew from my years as an environmental educator that river pollution is caused by people who don't understand the dynamics of water. Used motor oil poured into street drains flows into the local stream. Septic systems leach into lakes. And, more often than not, the polluter is unaware of the pollution because of a lack of understanding about watersheds.

So, I was not completely surprised that my kids didn't understand rivers, but I was determined that they would not be the unknowing polluters of tomorrow and that today a new understanding of water would begin to permeate their worldview.

Now the class circled the sandbox looking puzzled and expectant and, without an explanation of what we were up to, I began giving directions. "Thomas and Jonah, would you please go into the downstairs boys' bathroom closet and get a whole role of plastic bags, the ones we use to line the trash cans? Reesa and Rebecca, would you please go up to the classroom and get a few pairs of scissors? I am sure I don't have to tell you how to walk with them. And, while you are there, could you go into our closet and get the three watering cans we used last year in the garden?"

As children ran back into the building in search of supplies, I wondered what had come over me. I was the teacher who planned everything, who got up early to hike in the woods before taking the class on the same walk. I was the teacher who spent hours each weekend writing detailed plans. Now, I was the teacher who was ignoring my lesson plan to undertake a project that I had not tested, a project that might not even work.

I continued asking students to gather the supplies we would need without telling them what we would be doing with the shovels, buckets, trowels and rocks. My kids were used to being led toward an understanding that began in a mystery, and were not surprised when my raised eyebrows and a smile comprised the silent answer to their questions about what we were doing. Finally, when the class and all the materials were gathered, I announced, "We're going to create a river in the sandbox."

More quickly than I thought possible, busy hands removed a foot of sand, laid down overlapping rows of the plastic bags to provide an impermeable layer of imitation bedrock and heaped the sand over the plastic bags to form hills and valleys. Now ten and eleven years old, my kids had long ago given up playing in this huge fifteen by thirty foot rectangular sandbox. But, their years of sandbox play were akin to my years as a professional environmentalist—a long preparation for our outdoor geography lesson.

"Now," I said, "it's time to make our river." Before I could give out the next bit of instruction, Andy picked up a stick and began to scratch a gully from one of the hills toward the plain. "Not so fast." I said, kneeling into our model and smoothing away all traces of this unnecessary groove.

"We are going to do this another way, the way it really happens in nature. Who do you think comes along with an enormous stick and makes a pathway for a river?"

I picked up the watering can and began sprinkling the landscape with rain showers. "All we are going to do," I said, "is make it rain."

Soon children ran to and from the lavatories, carrying watering cans. The first rain shower soaked into the sand. The second and the third downpour eroded small stream beds that flowed together to create a growing artery system across the hills. The artificial rainstorms flowed down these courses and then, at the bottom of the hills, sunk into the land. Children, excited by the prospect of creating a flowing river, ran back inside the school for more water. We found buckets and filled these too and poured them through the watering cans in perpetual showers that drenched the hills, the valleys and the plains. The hillside stream beds grew deeper and wider and a network of empty waterways traversed the plains. But, each time it rained, the water flowed briefly along these channels then soaked quickly into the sand. We made rain for ten minutes, twenty minutes, and still we did not have a flowing river.

I began to doubt my decision. Perhaps this would not work. Maybe the water was not forming an aquifer, a waterlogged layer of sand above the imitation bedrock, but was seeping between the plastic bags. Perhaps we would never see a flowing river. And, it seemed, we certainly would never see a river form and fall over the edge of the plain into the deep basin at the edge of the sandbox that the class had designated the ocean.

I had hoped to wrap up work on our impromptu river model by the end of Main Lesson. But, now it was time for snack and there was still no river. I sent Evan and Rebecca and Thomas inside to bring out all the lunch boxes. Children took turns eating, running for water and making rain. Soon, children from other classes poured out of the building for recess. We apologized for taking over their sandbox. They stood around and watched. Helen said proudly, "we are making a river."

I wondered if we were.

Other teachers joined us too. They told me about loud children who had been running up and down the halls in violation of the no running in the halls rule. They told me about the puddles on the floor that a kind teacher had mopped up. I apologized while thinking that not only was this going to be a poorly-planned model of a dry waterbed of a non-existent river, it was starting to get me into hot water with my colleagues who might not appreciate the actual rivers running out of the boys and girls lavatories into the hall.

Recess ended and I sent the fifth graders to their handwork lesson and continued making rain with fourth graders. A shallow lake formed. We kept making rain. The departure of the fifth graders lowered our numbers and signaled a change in spirit. Now the polite, yet pointed, questions and statements began.

"Mrs. Allsup, do you know this will actually work?"

""How long do we have to do this?"

"My arms hurt."

Worthwhile efforts often call us to persevere beyond the reasonable point of surrender. Just as I began to consider giving up, it happened. We could not see it, but the sand reached the point of saturation. Suddenly, tributaries filled, the lake ejected a stream that dug its own bed and inched its way toward the ocean. Everyone cried out at once.

"Look! It's happening!"

"It's a river."

"More water, fast!

"Run!"

"Keep making it rain!"

"Look it's going to reach the ocean."

"The whole thing is flowing!"

Children ran, children poured. Arms, tired of holding the heavy watering cans, passed the heavy vessels, still pouring, to other arms.

Then we stopped making the rain. And, like a miracle, for long, breath-holding seconds, the river continued to flow.

Years ago, when it had been recommended that I teach two grade levels, I had hesitated. Knowing that there would be problems I could not anticipate, I had, nevertheless, agreed to merge the new first graders with my original class. Now, I had managed a combined class for more than three years and, on most days, I was barely aware that there was anything unusual about the juggling I did to make it all work.

But today I had dropped the ball. Building a river had taken far longer than I had anticipated. The heavy green doors of the building opened and the fifth graders flowed silently down the steps toward the jubilant fourth graders.

"You should have seen it."

"It was awesome"

"We stopped making the rain happen and the river kept going. It was just like a real river."

The big moment had come and gone and the fifth graders had missed it.

I saw disappointment in the faces of the older class, but, good sports, they helped to remove the thick layer of sand, pull out the plastic bags and return the sand box to its original purpose—a training ground for future geography students. Climbing the stairs with my wet, sandy mob, carrying lunch boxes, pails, watering cans and wads of wet sandy plastic bags, I realized that I could not wait to discuss our experience. The usual plan was to let students digest what they had learned by holding off a discussion about their experience until the next day. But, if I was going to redeem anything for the fifth graders, I had to wrap them into the excitement of discovery that propelled sixteen fourth grade feet up the stairs.

Children washed hands and put things away. I thought about our upcoming conversation. I remembered my own childhood confusion about rivers. The way I saw it, the word "source" was where it all went wrong. One day in grade school my teacher had pointed to a blue speck on a big map and said, "Lake Itaska is the source of the Mississippi River." This statement was not followed by a demonstration in the sandbox or even a lecture on the dynamics of water systems. I was left with an image of a relatively small lake providing enough water to fill a mile-wide, thousand-mile-long river. Somehow, even as a child, I knew that this picture was incomplete, that I didn't understand rivers.

The fourth and fifth graders expected this to be their reading class. "Don't take out your books," I said. "I want to ask you something."

I paused and slowly repeated the question that had led to our impromptu demonstration.

"So, now that you have made a river, can you tell me why the Mississippi River can't be on Cape Cod, on this side of the canal?"

Answers gushed from my fourth and fifth graders, fast rushing answers.

"There is just not enough land"

"Or enough rain."

"A big river needs a lot of little rivers to flow into it and it would take a lot of space for all those small rivers…"

"Tributaries, they are called," I said

"Right, tributaries, to flow together."

"Cape Cod is just way too small."

"That's it!" I said. "Exactly. Cape Cod is just way too small. When I was a student, my teacher told me that rivers have a source, a certain lake perhaps. What would you say is the source, the beginning of a river?"

"I don't see how you can say it's a lake."

"It's everywhere."

"Yeah, it rains everywhere."

"The everywhere for a river is called its watershed," I said. "Bays have watersheds too. For instance, because rain on street next to the school flows into the canal, we are in the watershed for Buzzards Bay and Cape Cod Bay. All the water that rains here ends up in the canal and, depending on which way the canal is flowing, goes to Buzzards Bay or Cape Cod Bay."

"And pollution…if you change the oil in your car and pour it down a street drain, where does it go?"

"Into a river."

"Or a bay."

"Wherever you are, it's in a watershed."

"That's right." I said, smiling.

The French teacher walked in, "Bonjour," she said

"Bonjour, Madame," I replied. And left my class to imagine watersheds in a country far away.

A thought came to me that night as I reflected on my bold and potentially foolhardy departure from the lesson plan, on coming to the brink of halting the experiment, on the thrill of seeing the river flow, on the fifth grader's disappointment, on the final clear understanding that had grown out of experience rather than a lecture.

If I had just explained the nature of rivers, it would have been like taking a big stick and carving an unnatural channel across the face of the land. But, making the model, offering an opportunity to learn through experience, was like making it rain. Like water falling gently on the hillsides, experience makes its own channels.

Someday, these children would leave this school, and I and all their other teachers would no longer be involved in shaping their daily learning experiences. And then, perhaps, after the metaphorical rain of experiential learning has stopped, great rivers of understanding would flow on their own.

20

Turning Point

...sometimes letting go is an act of far greater power than defending or hanging on.
—Eckhart Tolle

A PICKUP TRUCK pulls into our campsite as Reesa and Diana, who are on the food prep team with me, set paper plates on two picnic tables while I feed dry spaghetti into boiling water. The rest of the class is down the road playing softball with two parents. Our camping field trip on the outer Cape is close enough that chaperones can come and go in shifts. Adrian, Jeremy's Dad, hauls boats for a living and he is arriving at the end of a day when we have hiked along Cape Cod Bay and he has completed the last leg of a long trek from Florida. We have a permit for a campfire at the beach. Adrian approaches the picnic tables announcing, "I remembered the firewood."

"I guess it's been a pretty long day for you," I said.

"You might say that," he said raising his eyebrows and nodding in a way that hinted he had a story to tell.

"I was making good time driving up the coast pulling this 40-foot sloop. Seems I am on the road all the time this spring. I promised Jeremy I would come on this trip and that I would be here in time for the campfire on the beach tonight, so I knew I had to keep making good time.

"I'm on ninety-five outside Baltimore in the early morning commute, bumper to bumper, just creeping, thinking to myself, much more of this snail's pace and I'm going to miss the marshmallow roast.

And then the truck stalls. I try to turn it over. Nothing. Try again. Nothing. So, I get out of the truck and open it up. I look everywhere but can't see the problem. Back in the cab. It still won't start. And now I hear this guy talking on the radio. He's talking about this huge traffic jam that goes on for miles. And I'm thinking, now I have that ahead of me too and once this thing starts, I'm never going to get through all of that in time. Then I notice the helicopters. Traffic helicopters. And the guy on the radio is saying, 'It's a big truck hauling a boat totally stopped in the middle of the highway. That's the cause of the traffic back up.' And it takes me a minute to realize that they're talking about me. That the traffic jam is behind me and that I am the cause of it.

"So I'm on the radio with Marsha and we're trying to figure out what to do." Marsha is Jeremy's Mom and she is the logistical genius behind the family boat hauling business. She is also the logistical genius behind our field trip, coordinating the coming and going of parents, food, and firewood. "I don't know how she did it, but she found someone to haul the truck and the boat to a garage."

It seems impossible that Adrian has had time for a truck repair and nine hours of driving from Baltimore to Eastham. But here he is, standing next to the spaghetti boiling on the camp stove under a pitch pine canopy, telling his story.

"And then Marsha says. 'You know how much this means to Jeremy.' And I say 'I promised him I would be there.' And so she finds me a flight into Providence. I left the boat right there on the highway. Marsha picked me up at the airport and I had just enough time to grab the firewood and get here for dinner."

Cars full of kids are pulling in to our campsite as he says this. Jeremy runs over to his Dad. I can't hear their short conversation, but see it is too brief for Adrian to give an account of his day.

Jeremy runs off with his friends unaware of how the efforts of his parents have made this moment so seamless, so perfect. And that is just how it should be, how it always has been. For, if we were to know, to truly realize in every moment all that our parents, our grandparents, our ancestors have done to make our lives possible, we would be paralyzed with gratitude.

Coast Guard Beach at twilight, with great combers folding, folding each in turn off to the horizon, down the long shore, where a century ago surfguards, seeking shipwrecks, walked miles along the frozen strand, bound to meet the next guard, turned and walked back into the windblown sand. My students know this history, about saving lives by hauling shipwrecked sailors and passengers suspended in air in a breeches buoy over the furious sea. They know all about how the loss of life along the Graveyard of the Atlantic led to the digging of the Cape Cod Canal whose ships we can see from our classroom windows. But now, on a late spring day, with the sun setting, the ghosts of history and the notion that this beach was once a fearsome place is far from their minds.

With bare feet and rolled up pants, a group of five children chase the receding waves into the sea, then, laughing, turn and run up the soft sand in advance of the next wave. The rest of the class helps to haul the firewood from Adrian's pickup, and, after building a crackling fire, leap in the growing darkness toward bright sparks that dance high in the breeze then flit, twinkling, off to the north. Nora, who has finished classes at the community college for the semester, and has joined us for part of the trip, strums her guitar until I gather the class around the campfire, and raising my voice to compete with the rising wind, tell a tall tale about Old Captain Stormalong.

Soon, the glowing embers call out for marshmallows and bright beams from flashlights lead searches for driftwood sticks.

Suddenly, out of the nearby darkness, a shriek, then a horrifying wail pierces the evening. It is Roland and he has stepped, barefoot, on a sharp piece of glass.

Adrian, a trained EMT, and Marc's Mom, a nurse, hover over him; the cut is deep and it bleeds profusely. While they decide whether to take Roland to the emergency room, I call the class to me. I am glad the children come quickly for, while the fire still glows, the night has become darker; the infinite ocean is now a menacing, roaring emptiness. Roland's moans mingle with the growing, groaning wind. The ghosts of the Graveyard of the Atlantic have been summoned by Roland's hearty wail.

We gather our gear, douse the fire, and I lead the class down a path to the friendly halo of a streetlight to wait for parents who have run to a distant parking lot to retrieve their vehicles. It has been determined that Roland does not need advanced medical care, but that he does need to get back to the campground where the cut can be examined in better light, disinfected and properly bandaged.

I am glad Adrian is with us. He had come for Jeremy and for his commitment to the class, but now it is Roland who needs him. Back in the campground, he takes charge of his care, exuding cheerfulness and confidence, shepherding Roland through the disinfection of the cut, and through the bedtime routine.

The rest of the trip has no unfortunate incidents. We enjoy an early morning bird walk, a hike up Pilgrim Monument, a visit to an Atlantic cedar swamp and the site of the telegraph station where Marconi first sent a wireless transatlantic message. And then, after an hour and a half car ride, we are back in our classroom with an eagerly awaited conversation on my mind.

I am usually keen to hear what my students remember, what they want to share after a field trip. And, this time I am especially interested in hearing them tell the tale of our evening at Coast Guard beach. I wonder whether they had felt it too.

The class enthusiastically tells about hikes and chores, about sleeping in tents and our pre-breakfast bird walk. Jeremy shares a bit of his Dad's tale. The class goes through the trip chronologically, skipping the evening at the beach.

"What about the evening at Coast Guard Beach?" I query.

"You mean when Roland stepped on the glass?" asked Rebecca.

"Yes," I nodded, "tell us about what happened then."

"It was strange," said Jonah.

"Yeah, really weird," said Marc.

"At first we had a lot of fun on the beach," added Diana.

"But then Roland screamed and all of a sudden it was really scary," said Philip.

"I couldn't wait to get out of there," said Reesa with an ominous tone.

"Yeah," said Andy, "we saw...."

There was a pause followed by nods, raised eyebrows, knowing looks and many voices speaking together, "We saw the elephant."

Whether it is caused by fear, a need for medical attention, a malfunctioning truck, or simply a sense that an experience has been completed, we all have moments when we are moving in one direction and then, unexpectedly, turn and take another course.

I did not know it yet, but in less than a year, I, like Adrian, would have to make a choice between doing what I expected to be doing in my job or doing what is right for my own child. Only, in my case, it would not be possible to return to a repaired truck in a few days and resume my journey.

This meant that at the end of the fifth and sixth grade year, three years before I had expected, I would leave my class. Now, at the end of our fourth and fifth grade year, a major life transition was only a year away, yet we had no sense that such a momentous change stood before us, that an elephant was about to round the corner.

21

Awakening

A single event can awaken within us a stranger
totally unknown to us. To live is to be slowly born.
  —Antoine de Saint-Exupery

I COULDN'T HELP smiling as I watched my new student, twelve-year-old William, running laps around the school field, one hand clutching his baggy pants to keep them from slipping inexorably toward his feet. This ten minute run was the energetic beginning of the two-hour class we called main lesson.

In spite of his trim, athletic physique, William ran in a lopsided and lackadaisical manner that, together with his ridiculously low-slung pants, had initially led me toward the admittedly judgmental conclusion that William's sloppiness in appearance probably meant carelessness in his character. But, I reassessed my initial impression after talking with his mother who revealed surprising details about William's morning ablutions and his painstaking selection of jeans and tee-shirts.

Now, as I looked more carefully, I saw that William actually worked hard to be impeccable. Immaculate from head to toe, he sported a practiced, bouncy walk and I learned from William himself that his wide-cut, low-slung trousers that exposed just a touch of plaid boxer shorts had been the Armani equivalent in his peer group at his previous school. I noticed that each hair was in place and that he wore the perfect combination of jewelry and a charming smile.

I tried to put myself in William's place when he joined our fifth and sixth grade class as a sixth grader, traveling toward our Cape Cod

151

school from his neighborhood just outside New Bedford, passing forests of white pine and an occasional flooded cranberry bog. Was he apprehensive each time he reached the apex of the Bourne Bridge, spotting our two-story brick building framed by trees in the foreground and Buzzard Bay and Vineyard Sound glistening in the distance? Did he pause before stepping out of the car to ask his mother for the umpteenth time why she had decided to separate him from his friends to send him to this school?

William was sociable with his classmates, but in class he seemed protected by a personal reserve. He did not participate in singing or group poetry recitation and he never raised his hand to offer an observation or an answer. Then, one day, unexpectedly, the class clown in him took a chance and he responded to a question with an impudent comment. By the end of the week his ability to execute a swift but temporary mutiny had won him a new position among his classmates. During our lessons, when he would offer a remark, all heads would turn and, for a flash, I would feel bereft as my authority was usurped by a charismatic twelve-year-old child.

I felt suddenly on shaky ground. I wasn't used to this. I knew that none of my long-term students would consider making an impolite remark in class. I knew this with certainty, for I knew my students well. Their tendencies, their proclivities, their academic and personal strengths and challenges had soaked into my consciousness over many years of lessons, recesses, class discussions, and personal conversations.

I had also taken up a more formal study of my students by learning how to observe students during group explorations called "Child Studies" in our weekly faculty meetings. Here we worked to discover the individuality of children and I came to see how important it was to notice such things as how each child walked and how tightly they gripped my hand in greeting every morning. It had been my job to lead my students on a path toward wonder, but my own wonder grew out of my growing understanding of each of them.

My observations during each school day continued to be deepened by an evening meditation on each child. Just before preparing my lesson for the following morning I would close my eyes and bring a picture of each student into my inner vision. Sometimes this would be a snapshot from our day together, and sometimes the image would be an inner impression, a sense of the child's developing soul. This contemplative attention had brought each child into my mind's eye night after night, year after year, until I felt him or her to be an integral part of my very being.

In contrast, I knew little about William. So I tried to play catch-up, to watch, to listen, to try to understand what worried him, what motivated him. I knew that William had learned how to be impeccable in a culture that valued loose jeans, gold chains and visible underwear. Now he was struggling to find some manner of comfort in what he termed a "weird school," in a room of kids with hopelessly unfashionable "tight pants," and a strange propensity for taking their teacher seriously.

Now, after five years with my class, my students had become like family. One of the many advantages of such a relationship was the ability to carry traditions and activities from one school year to the next. One of the class's favorite non-competitive games involved standing in a circle and creating and solving math problems in a rhythmic sequence. The first child might offer "five times" and the next child might say "three is" and the third child had to answer "fifteen" while keeping the beat. The next student might say "twenty minus," then the next child "thirteen is" and the answering person said "seven." The rhythm was supported by finger snapping by all, and, when we were on a roll, knees would bounce, shoulders sway and smiles would erupt as a student looked perplexed, and then gave the right answer just in time to keep the rhythm going. We played this number game round and round the circle for many minutes during each main lesson.

It hadn't always been this smooth. When we started this daily activity during the previous school year, we were far from rhythmic. Some number facts seemed elusive. Certain students were weak on the higher times tables. Often students didn't pay close attention and did not hear their cues. Our progress had lurched along unevenly. We laughed, then fixed mistakes. Everyone worked on becoming more focused. Memories improved. By the end of that year we had become good at this number game. My kids never spoke of their sense of accomplishment, but a few weeks after William joined us in the fall of 1996, they returned my confident smile one fall morning when I said, "five times" and turned to my neighbor.

I asked William to watch until he understood the rules. He knew his number facts, but, when he stepped into the circle, he refused to attempt the rhythmic pattern that made this activity so much fun. He could often be seen bouncing down the hall to the beat of a whispered rock song, so I knew that his rhythmic sensibilities went far beyond what was required for this simple math game. But, when it was his turn, he did not pick up the beat. Instead, he paused, looked at his feet and our group dynamic slowed until he muttered the correct number, then resumed again. William's attitude here reminded me of his sloppy approach to running. However, now that I had moved beyond judging, I saw that William wasn't careless. He was embarrassed. This odd activity was not cool at all. I could see now that, for William, the only saving thing was that his friends from his old school were not watching him play this silly game.

I was concerned that the class might be impatient with William for messing up our hard earned arithmetical perfection. So, I was relieved when they offered him understanding, generous smiles. I also carried this patient, protective gesture toward William. Above all, I wanted to spare him any additional embarrassment. So, while I freely offered advice and suggestions to my long-term students, I did not share most of my critique of William's work, his manner or his behavior. This forbearance had the affect of increasing my attention. Each time I held back a suggestion that William join us in singing, restrained a reprimand about looking out the window, or withheld an invective about actually listening to the twenty-five minute lessons I delivered from memory each day, my awareness of William intensified so that, over time, William came to occupy much of my attention.

An observer in my classroom might have judged me to be too complacent about William's lack of progress, might think I had given up on him. Perhaps an experienced teacher watching me with William would have thought my approach to him was lazy or incompetent. I knew this because an impatient voice in my own mind questioned everything I did and, in William's case, everything I did not do.

This voice prodded me to impose plans that would quickly bring William into compliance. It asked, "Shouldn't you consider tutoring? Don't you remember the educational psychology class you took as an undergraduate? Wouldn't behavior modification, a carefully designed system of rewards, be the best way to reach a kid like William who comes from a very different schooling environment? Shouldn't you start now by showering praise on William each time you notice a small success? Why not try to compliment each slight improvement in handwriting or give him a smile and a pat on the back for a correct answer to a math problem? Shouldn't you call his parents to enlist their help in motivating William through punishments and incentives? Can you really expect that a twelve-year-old, who is already a rebel against all things academic, will, on his own, without intense prodding of some sort, evolve, perhaps magically, into an eager learner?"

This impatient inner voice that wanted me to do something active to prod William argued constantly with my inner impulse toward patient observation and threw in a measure of guilt to make sure I was paying attention. However, my patient tendencies ruled with stubborn determination. I justified my laconic approach by recalling another student's challenging transition into our class culture.

Jeremy had come to our class the previous year, at the start of fourth grade, with wide eyes, an easy smile, and a willingness to participate that matched the intensity of William's reluctance. Jeremy was a natural at all sports, and, within his first week, had become an integral member of the group that streamed down the stairs and out to the kickball game at the bottom of the recess hill.

Teachers at Jeremy's past school had seen him as a well-adjusted achiever, and I too had come to appreciate his stunning academic competence. But I had worried about Jeremy almost as much as I now worried about William.

William had a habit of shunning all but minimum involvement in the teacher-defined aspects of our school. In his previous school he had invested himself in peer-defined contests regarding dress and behavior, including scorn for teachers and the work they assigned. In contrast, Jeremy had learned how to work steadily and successfully in all subjects.

While William was likely to tip his chair back, stare out the window, then glance at a blank notebook, Jeremy had leaned over his desk, muscles tense, his hand moving steadily across the page. In his quiet, focused concentration he was similar to most of my long-term students. The room silent, with everyone sinking into concentration, Jeremy would raise his hand. I would motion to him to bring his notebook to the front of the room where I knew he would say something that I rarely heard from my other pupils. Laying the book on my desk, he always uttered the same words, "Is it good?"

It was always good, really good.

While his classmates worked steadily without seeking my approval, Jeremy asked for my evaluation many times each day. He was used to gold stars, letter grades, and frequent praise. Seeing that Jeremy felt lost without such supports, I gave him the encouragement he needed. But I hoped that, like his classmates, he would soon find that learning provides its own rewards.

It was Jeremy's research for a report about the ginkgo tree that led to a transformation. I never knew whether it was the medicinal properties of the gingko leaves, the fact that the tree is its own species, the unusual shape of the leaves, or all of this together that was the spark that ignited Jeremy's interest. He convinced his parents to help him buy and plant a gingko tree in their yard and, as he delivered his oral report, I heard a new eagerness in his voice. When he finished speaking, he appeared satisfied. He did not ask," Is this good?"

I wanted William to discover the gift of wonder and to find that he could feel engaged in learning. I wanted him to have his own equivalent of Jeremy's ginkgo tree. I did not want to replace William's apathy with an orientation towards rewards, with a feeling that he worked for me rather than for himself. Yet, it was clear that William's ginkgo equivalent would never be found if he continued to seclude himself in his own private world during class time.

During my daily storytelling, William appeared to be unmovable. He didn't laugh at the funny parts or react to dramatic moments. He never volunteered to take part in our tradition of reviewing the story the day after it was told. In the early grades the children usually simply retold the story. Now they were able to condense the story or lesson fairly quickly, then discuss what it meant to them. William's wooden demeanor during even the most heated discussions convinced me that, even when our conversation sparked with intense controversy, he wasn't listening.

During the previous school year, Jeremy had made most of his transition into our culture of eager learning over a couple of months. By Thanksgiving I had all but forgotten that he was new to our class. This year, William's wooden participation had gone on from September through January, through our review of fractions and long division, through Gautama Buddha, many pharaohs, Gilgamesh, the Fertile Crescent, through Odysseus, the parts of speech, through Athens and Sparta. In midwinter he showed no signs of engaging in the substance of our work and I began to wonder whether he would ever get anything out of his time in our class.

My sense of guilt became palpable. My impatient inner voice said, "I told you so," and came close to overpowering my impulse to protect William from pressure. I began to think that it was probably too late for William to allow himself to become interested in history, math, or science. After all, he had devoted too many years to learning disengagement, to developing an oppositional relationship to teachers, and, as a result, he was likely to be so set in his ways that he could not change without energetic interventions.

My husband had often laughed at the unrealistic optimism that surfaced in me when approaching almost any difficulty. He had even made up his own aphorism that he used when he thought I was being too naïve about the likelihood of success in the face of a daunting problem. Now my impatient voice taunted me with his words. Thinking of my too-little-too-late approach to William, I said to myself, "You really did believe that daisies might grow out of the floor."

It was not only my pig-headed optimism that had caused me to believe that William might, somehow, experience an academic awakening. My graduate school training in the philosophy behind Waldorf education and my five years of classroom experience had steeped me in a perspective antithetical to the behavior modification which

I studied as an undergraduate and which stands behind so much of current practice in schooling today. B.F. Skinner, the most famous practitioner of behaviorism, had shown that it is possible to use his methods to teach just about anything to anyone and had demonstrated this by training pigeons to play ping pong. Food was the reward he provided for each step the pigeons took toward ping pong playing. Similarly, a behavioristic approach to human learning provides rewards for defined behaviors, typically in the form of praise and grades.

Those who have invested themselves in this popular paradigm for motivating students have lost sight of the fact that learning is to the soul as food is to the body. Learning is a journey into fantastic new information, amazing skills, and a growing sense of mastery. Children don't need external rewards to influence them to be naturally drawn into wondrous experiences and the sense of amazement that comes with growing competence. If the appropriate experience is given at the right time and if children are not distracted by praise and extrinsic rewards, the process of learning engenders a sense of awe, which is the soul's self-administered reward.

Being a teacher who works consciously with wonder is a lot like being a cook. The art and science of creating an appealing, nourishing meal is similar to the art and science of creating an engaging lesson. To a large extent, knowing the inner needs that are common at each developmental age helps a teacher choose material that will be both nourishing and appealing. Beyond this, just as a parent comes to know the food preferences of all members of the family, truly understanding the interests, learning style, and temperament of each child helps a teacher prepare lessons that are both rewarding and nourishing.

Such was the inner talk of my patient self, the voice that was, now, in mid-winter, beginning to sound good in theory but useless in practice. Theory aside, so much of the year had gone by and William had apparently made little progress. Now, my other voice, the impatient voice that had been pushed into the background, stepped forward and announced that what worked for my long term students would not work for William. It was too bad he had not come to our school in first grade and grown in our culture. If I had been more realistic from the start, if I had gone after William's attention with a bit more vehemence, with the same approach Skinner used with the pigeons, perhaps William would, by now, engage in our work in a productive manner. It was as if my long-term students and I were taking a long journey by ship and it was my fault that, in the parlance of the controversial education law, William was being left behind.

As we approached the end of our Greek history block, I realized we were running behind in my curriculum plan. When I do my planning in the summer, I always leave one or two spare, unplanned lessons each month. This way I have flexibility. The detailed research behind each lesson happens the week I am telling it, usually the night before. Sometimes I discover an additional biography that calls out to be told, or I find that the class needs an engaging story to enliven their comprehension of a new concept.

This January, snow days and my diversions had used up the couple of spare days and more. I needed to leave Greece and return to our study of decimals, but I had to do justice to Philip and to his son Alexander. And how would I fit in Demosthenes, the Greek orator who put pebbles in his mouth to perfect his speaking? I decided I could save time by clumping Philip and his rival Demosthenes into one lesson before moving on to a multi-day story about Alexander the following day.

Ready to tell the story of Demosthenes and Philip, I stood quietly before my class of fifteen students in our spacious but drafty class-room. In spite of the many challenges that come with living inside an antique, we loved this almost century old building with its expansive windows and its view of the Bourne Bridge and the upper decks of the largest ships on the canal.

In many ways, the building was like our curriculum, old but good. Interpreting this venerable curriculum in an antique school building makes me feel that I have stepped outside of our high speed, multi-tasking, media-driven electronic age and into a more grounded era. Here, a sense of timelessness envelops the perpetual stream of child-hood and provides a platform for taking the leap to bygone ages, today a leap to ancient Greece.

Outside the window I see the Bourne Bridge and cars moving across it ant-like toward Cape Cod. Everyone but William looks at me expectantly. We are ready for that leap. Then the room is gone, the bridge is gone, and we are in Athens looking at a seven-year-old boy who has just lost his father and has been turned over to greedy guard-ians who steal his inheritance so that he cannot attend school. I am seeing, and more importantly, feeling the story of Demosthenes and transforming that seeing and feeling into words.

"One day Demosthenes went to a courtroom where he listened to a lawyer try to convince more than a thousand jurymen of his point of view. Demosthenes found himself listening so intently that he lost track of time. One hour, then two, then three went by and still he listened. He watched the jurymen listen too. He saw them lean for-ward with interest and look sad or happy as the orator carried them with the power of his voice. Demosthenes decided that he too would become a lawyer. He went home and began to study right away. He worked so hard that, in only a year's time, he was able to bring suit against his guardians and win back much of his inheritance.

"Soon after he won his case, he made a public speech. He knew his facts, but he mumbled his words and spoke in a flat, uninteresting voice. He was such a poor speaker that people laughed at him. Even his friends said, 'Demosthenes, you had better find a new type of work.'

"Demosthenes walked the streets of Athens with his shoulders slumped and his head hung low. He was close to giving up. But a small voice deep in his soul told him that he could be a great orator someday if he was willing to work hard to improve himself.

"He set himself to work right away. He knew he had to stop mumbling, but how? And how was he to speak loudly enough to be heard over the roar of a large group of people? He had an idea. He went to the beach where the sounds of the waves roared more loudly than the crowds. He bellowed until the far off gulls could hear him and his throat grew sore. But that was not enough. He reached down and gathered pebbles and put these in his mouth. He tried to speak clearly with the pebbles. At first his mumbling was even worse. But he kept at it and soon his voice was clear even with the pebbles. He practiced like this for days."

I paused for a moment to gather thoughts about how Demosthenes did become a great public speaker and how he spoke out against Philip. I thought about transitioning to Philip's story. Then I noticed something.

William was listening.

Demosthenes, who worked so hard to reach his fellow Greek citizens with his voice, had now reached across the ages to speak to William. And I, who had long practiced the potentially overly optimistic impulse to watch and wait, and had recently come to the brink of giving in to my impatient voice, felt my heart quicken as William took this small, almost secret step toward participation.

I had held back my active management of William for so long

that now my entire consciousness, including the patient observer, and my impatient voice, united in a heightened awareness of William and an intention to do whatever I could to sustain his attention. I looked out the window, appearing, I hoped, to enter into a normal pause in storytelling. Actually, this was not a normal pause at all but a moment to create a radical reconstruction of my lesson. Pushing Philip into the next day's story, I searched my memory for more about Demosthenes, the parts of the story I had planned to leave out just to make time.

Stealthily, I watched William as I told about how Demosthenes built a special practice room below ground where he could work on his skills without interruption. William looked up with interest as I told about how Demosthenes realized that he left the room too often to make good progress, so he shaved half his head to force himself to stay in the room because he would be too embarrassed to be in public. I could see William was still with me as I recounted how Demosthenes hung a sword over the shoulder that he tended to raise when speaking.

It was a barely perceptible change, William's listening. It was like the first sounds of late winter snowmelt, a slow drip from the roof that softly signals the rush of spring.

His classmates had not noticed.

That evening I considered why it was Demosthenes who had caught William's attention. Perhaps it was that Demosthenes and William were truly kindred spirits. Like Demosthenes, William was deeply self-conscious and easily embarrassed and was willing to work hard to gain approval from his peers. Appearance was important to both of them; they both wished to be impeccable. They both wanted to influence others.

Someone who believes that daisies can grow through the floor might imagine that a disaffected student who finally listened to a lesson might already be prepared to take another step. Perhaps the next morning would find William ready to join in our conversation about Demosthenes. Holding a glorious picture in my mind of William's open, interested gaze, I wondered whether he was ready to take a big leap. Would he be brave enough to speak about Demosthenes in front of the class?

I usually call on volunteers to help retell the previous day's story, but sometimes I choose a student who has not offered to speak. In spite of the inner movement I had witnessed in William, I guessed he would not volunteer to talk about what he had heard. I wanted to call on him, but I was concerned about putting him on the spot too soon. Perhaps he would be too embarrassed to participate. I imagined him freezing up in front of the class and retreating ever deeper, even farther into himself.

I decided I would follow my instincts in the morning.

Addressing the whole class, I began, "Today you will tell me about a famous orator from Athens." William was looking at me. I took a deep breath and took his open gaze as an invitation.

"William," I said softly, but surely, "would you come up to the front of the room?" He walked up and I smiled at him as I sat down in his chair. He looked comfortable as he smiled bemusedly at his classmates.

"William, I'd like you to tell us what you remember about Demosthenes."

"Who's that?" he shot back with a wrinkled brow.

Oh no, I thought, I've done it now. My impatient voice, my guilt, has teamed up with my tendency to be overly optimistic and now I have pushed William too far, too fast. I was not the only one in the room who thought I might have put too much pressure on William. His classmates, who thought I was breaking our unspoken rule about going easy on William, appeared concerned and confused. In their silence, in their questioning looks, I could hear them saying, "How could you put him on the spot like this?"

I ignored their consternation and my own fears and, optimistically, continued speaking to William: "The man I talked about yesterday who wanted to become a good speaker, who went to the beach to practice his speaking."

"Oh! that guy!" he said with confident recognition.

Speaking as if he had always stood before the class, immersed in the retelling of a story, William, with a few prompts from me, told us about all the things Demosthenes did to himself, the pebbles, the head shaving, the sword hung above his shoulder. I had the sense he was talking about an admired popular figure rather than a long-dead Greek orator. I watched the class as he spoke. I had known for a full day that William was with us. And now, as William stood before the class speaking with confidence about another person who learned how to speak with confidence, his classmates surreptitiously shared surprised looks while he smashed the image they held of an impeccable, charismatic rebel, an outsider who had captivated our attention but had not truly entered into the life of the class. Optimism, faithful waiting, and quiet attention had bought William the time he needed to awaken into our academic journey.

William finished speaking and walked back to his seat as I returned to my place in the front of the room. As he sat down his classmates burst into joyful applause. He smiled a broad, satisfied grin.

William was on board.

22

Healing

Love is not love that alters when it alteration finds.
—William Shakespeare

"I AM *not* wearing a skirt."

"It's a toga, William, not a skirt, and all the men wore these in ancient Greece."

"Maybe they did. But I'm not gonna."

"Well, you don't have to just yet. We're still in rehearsals. It will be weeks before the play. We'll see how you feel about it then."

William's response was a raised eyebrow and an expression that combined a sneer and a grunt.

The other boys began wearing togas to rehearsals and one day William appeared wearing his. Like his friends, he wore a pair of white gym shorts under the toga. I knew this because he continually adjusted his clothing so that the hem of these shorts just barely stuck out under the putative skirt. William had devised a compromise; with the shorts peeking out beneath the toga, he seemed to be wearing short pants and a long white shirt. And he had made his contribution to fashion history.

The visible undergarment was, at least in our class, an accepted part of ancient Greek attire.

Retelling the story of Demosthenes had indeed been a turning point for William. Over the next month, he began learning how to write his own compositions, and he attempted to keep the rhythm in our number games. One day, I noticed him covertly joining in during singing and speech work. After a few weeks of tentative participation in this choral work, he seemed to realize that nobody would make fun of him and he increased his volume. William's unsolicited remarks became less frequent and more appropriate and sometimes were so funny that I joined the class in laughter.

I still gave William extra time in my evening meditations. But now the images that came to me when I pictured him brought less worry and more hope.

As I watched William in rehearsals for our class play, I reflected on how far he had come since September when he had all but refused to participate in a classroom skit. During the first weeks of school when he was new to the class, I had used part of a classical tale from India, the Ramayana, to teach about that culture's belief in reincarnation. We had made lists of the characters from the loftiest, the young prince Rama, to the least exalted, a dog. Each day we had a new cast of characters as students had imagined their reincarnation into a new life.

William had been uncomfortable. In September, performing in an impromptu play had been too embarrassing. Getting him to leave his seat and stand with the class while I said his lines was the best we could do.

By the second week it had seemed to me that we had pulled all potential value out of this exercise. It had sparked some meaningful conversations about reincarnation. ("Who says the dog is the least exalted character? Maybe he is the most.") The part where prince Rama is prevented from becoming king had initiated thoughtful conversations about the ability to adjust to unexpected changes. It seemed we could not learn anything more from continuing our daily dramatic performance. And it was taking a lot of time. I told the class we would stop doing the skit.

"But we haven't all had a chance to play every role," said Reesa.

"I thought that tomorrow I would get to be the dog," said Jonah.

The pleading had continued with everyone except William begging to perform the skit every day until each child had performed every role. I had given in to the rest of the class. William's classmates began saying his lines for him. I sat back and enjoyed watching the class improve and strengthen this ten-minute performance like a seasoned acting troupe. The long-term members of the class had been in their glory. William had been in agony.

Now, seven months later, here was William preparing for our class play, dressing for rehearsals, remembering his cues, saying his lines, adjusting his hemline so his shorts would show, moving according to stage directions, adjusting his hem again.

One day, a week before performing our play, William took another step in his role as a Greek student in our adaptation of *The Clouds* by Aristophanes. With no warning, he gave us an interpretation of his character as a bumbling fool. We all roared with laughter and I encouraged him to use his inspired silliness in our play.

But, during our performance for an audience, he was not confident enough to act the part of a fool, was not yet ready to take a chance at appearing ridiculous before older students and his parents. He had come a long way, though, and I was happy that he had appeared on stage, delivered lines and worked cooperatively with his classmates.

I found myself thinking that we had much work to do together. I had a flash of William a year older. Another year, I thought, would bring a further dwindling of William's tendency toward easy embarrassment. In another year he might be able to write longer compositions, might finally let go of his suspicion that, as a teacher, I must be the enemy.

❦

I was used to picturing my kids a year older, to contemplating how to help them, to seeing them as a part of my life through eighth grade. But something had happened. Now, I was going to have to shake that habit of seeing myself as the teacher of my beloved class.

Because there wasn't going to be another year.

By September Nora's headaches had diminished enough that she had been ready to go back to school. She had left home for a Waldorf boarding school in New Hampshire and there, in October, her headaches had changed from one day trials into three day ordeals. It had not been possible to sleep away her headaches in the noisy dormitory. We had decided that she would come home for the balance of the year, but that we would move to New Hampshire over the next summer so she could go back to school the following year and not have to live in a dormitory.

My fellow teachers knew all of this. They would hold the secret of my unexpected departure as long as they could. But soon they would have to advertise for a new teacher. Before they placed ads, I would have to tell the parents. I would have to tell my students.

All over the world teachers said goodbye to classes at the end of the year. But not here. Here we expected to remain a family through eighth grade.

Rudolf Steiner told teachers that it was essential that they love their students. He saw love as a "vivifying, creative, transmuting power." He did not put curriculum standards, test scores or college acceptance rates at the center of his picture of schooling. Love is at the center.

I did not spend time doubting our decision to move for the sake of keeping Nora in high school in spite of her health challenges. But I had not figured out how to live with the prospect of leaving my class. At home I slept poorly and cried easily. This was not the life I had ever imagined, a life in which I would leave my students, leave our school, leave Cape Cod.

Jeremy had been helped by the gingko tree and William had found a soul mate in Demosthenes. During my years with my class, I had seen many instances in which a story helped a child understand something or cope with change. Sometimes I had made up special pedagogical stories to lift a child to a new vision. Now, as I began to grieve over leaving my class, I kept coming back to a story that had been a centerpiece of our autumn study of ancient India—the Ramayana.

In my mind's eye, I pictured the skit we had practiced daily in September. I saw Rama, the favored prince who everyone in the kingdom thought would be chosen to be their leader. Once, in a battle, Rama's father, Dasaratha, the king, lost a chariot wheel. After his youngest wife repaired the chariot, he offered her two favors. She asked to save these boons for another day. The king agreed to this and then his promise moved to the back of his mind.

Years later she reminds the king of his promise. He prepares to grant her wish. But, when she informs him that her wish is to have her own son, not Rama, take the throne, the king is devastated.

He knows he has to fulfill his promise to her. He stays up all night, distraught because Rama, his favored son, will not be king. He paces and worries and wishes this turn of events had not happened. This inner fighting with destiny is a sign that the king is not an exalted being. In our ordering of merit in our reincarnation list, we had placed the king near the bottom, near the demanding wife, near the dog. I know that my inability to feel positive about a new vision for my future shows I am like Rama's father. I see my inner work is to try to become more like Rama himself.

When the king visits Rama to tell him that he will not become king and that he is to be banished, Rama accepts his fate with pure equanimity and begins to prepare for his journey. When I think of this story, I focus on this moment, on Rama's understanding nod, on his calm acceptance, his practice of the ancient wisdom of non-attachment. No tears, no hair tugging, no gnashing of teeth, just a calm re-orientation to a new view of the future. Now, with my vision of our future transformed by an unexpected misfortune, this story helps me get through my days. I concentrate on flowing with destiny, on letting go of my picture of the future so that I can focus on lessons, on students, on each moment.

Yet, in the evenings, my grief returns and I reflect on whether I am completely in tune with Rama's ancient wisdom. Rama, who was a mythological figure, and Buddha, an historical person, both taught that we can live in a place above pain through non-attachment, that we can love in a way that implies no ownership. Their teachings encourage us to live wholly in the moment and to accept that all things, even our deep connections with our loved ones, are temporary. While these ideas and Rama's story help me get through my school days, I find that the principle of non-attachment is not enough.

When I am alone, and I do not have to accomplish the tasks of teaching or parenting, I come back to the wisdom my friend and colleague had given me when Nora's headaches first began to redefine our days: "Learn to live with the sadness." Her advice was based on the idea that the most important goal is not contentment. So I let go of Rama at night, and sit alone in the dark on the sofa, meditate on each of the dear children in my class and enter into the sadness of leaving them.

The next morning I will wake with Rama in my thoughts.

For a time my days and nights existed in opposition to each other. I floated between two philosophies of being. During the day I let go of images of the future and lived in the present. At night, I entered a dark cave where I yearned for Nora's health, where I already missed my students, where I cried.

Over time, however, I came to I realize that my days and nights were not opposing sides of a duality, but two unified aspects of coping. Feeling the depths of my sadness is an important part of adjusting to the future. But Rama's help, his focus on the present, is also part of coping. This is the lesson I had learned from Marc after he broke his leg in first grade. The pain is real and cannot be ignored, but resilience means not allowing our difficulties to prevent us from finding joy in our days.

23

Compassion

A human being is part of a whole, called by us the Universe, a part limited in time and space. He experiences himself, his thoughts and feelings, as something separated from the rest—a kind of optical delusion of his consciousness. This delusion is a kind of prison for us, restricting us to our personal desires and to affection for a few persons nearest us. Our task must be to free ourselves from this prison by widening our circles of compassion to embrace all living creatures and the whole of nature in its beauty.
—Albert Einstein

I WANTED TO WORK with math in a way that was new to the class, the seat-of-the-pants kind of math that lets us estimate the number of miles we drove on a trip, how much the week's groceries might cost, how many people live in our neighborhood. I figured we would do it by designing a city.

I hoped that this would be more than an exercise, a problem that could have been in a math book. I hoped that we would be pushing into a new territory, finding an inkling of the type of adult wonder known to researchers, to city planners, to all who are responsible for seeing and changing the face of the earth. This would be far from the wide-eyed seven-year-old innocent awe. It would be a more mature amazement arising from our human capacity to create magnificence.

"Let's imagine that we are going to design a completely new city. When I was a child, the country of Brazil built a new capital called Brasilia. It was a completely new, planned city, built all at once. Most cities develop slowly over time. But planned cities are different. The city planners decide from the start how many people will live there, how the transportation system will work, how many schools and universities there will be."

"Our city can have anything in it that you want, but it has to make mathematical sense. In order to do this, we are going to work with numbers in a new way. We are going to do a lot of thoughtful guessing. We are going to make a lot of estimates. We will work on this for a few weeks. Once we have all of our planning done we will draw maps of the city."

Abe raised his hand. New to the class this year, and not aware that he was about to suggest an activity that would be frowned upon by any Waldorf teacher, he forged ahead with his proclamation.

"I know what I want it to have," he exclaimed, "a video arcade in every neighborhood!" Abe smiled broadly, proud to have thought of this first, great suggestion and looked toward his friends for approval.

The reaction of the class was strong, yet, if I had not known these children since they were six years old, I might not have seen it. Abe didn't. He wasn't aware of the hidden half-smirks, the straightening of posture, and the flashing glances between classmates that signaled that something important was about to happen.

Mrs. Allsup had said that the city could include anything. Now, she was being tested. Now she would be changing her mind and making a list of disallowed features, the stuff that she did not approve of. There would be a challenge. Someone would say, "But you said." It would be interesting.

However, all I said was, "OK, but we have to see if the math works."

William, also a connoisseur of video arcades, blurted, "What does this have to do with math? You said the city could have anything we wanted."

Jonah joined in, "Really, you don't think we should have a video arcade."

"Well I do admit that I would rather see children reading books and riding bicycles than going to video arcades. But, I'm not going to say you can't have them. What we have to figure out is how much money the children in the city actually might have to use at a video arcade.

"Let's start with how much money you have. I am going to pass out paper. On the top, write down how much money you get each week from all sources, paper route, allowance, work for your parents that they pay you for. Then, under that, write how much you would like to spend at a video arcade."

I had planned to create a broad overview of the city in that lesson, but it seemed that we were about to focus on video arcades.

We collected the numbers and added and averaged and came up with about three dollars per fourth and fifth grade child per week that could be devoted to supporting a video arcade. I knew this was a high number, inflated by the high level of interest sparked by our conversation. Next, we calculated how much it would cost to set up the arcade, how much for rent, how much for employees, how much for profit. Finally, we had a number that told us how many children it would take to support a video arcade.

"This still doesn't tell us how many children there will be in the city and how many video arcades we can afford. We still don't know how many people will live in our city and how many of those people might be children and teenagers who might go to a video arcade. We will have to come back to that tomorrow. Meanwhile, I need you to do some homework that will help us come up with the numbers we need.

"Tomorrow, bring in a list of all the numbers of people in the households of your extended family. I mean grandparents, aunts, uncles and cousins. Write down the names and ages of everyone 22 and under, that is everyone who might be in school and also little kids too young to be in school. In addition to planning for video arcades, we will need these numbers to help us plan for schools."

The next day everyone had their lists. As we reviewed the numbers I felt a mood of open anticipation, a prelude, I hoped, for our sense of accomplishment in completing the whole project. I was glad to see that Abe and William were not only still on board, but they appeared to be the most focused students in the class that day, for, above all, they wanted to get to that ultimate number, how many video arcades our city could have.

I began with an attempt to calculate the numbers I had hoped to work with on our first day.

"We have to decide how big our city will be, closer to the size of Boston or closer to the size of, say, Providence. Raise your hand if you have ever been to Boston." Everyone raised a hand.

"Raise your hand if you have ever been to Providence."

Almost everyone raised a hand.

"When we went to the zoo, it was in Providence," I whispered with a smile.

The rest of the hands went up.

"Now, Boston has a population of about 600,000 and Providence has a population of about 150,000. First of all, these numbers are an example of estimating. Providence doesn't have exactly 150,000 people and Boston doesn't have exactly 600,000 people. It would be hard to get an exact number. Everyday people are born and people die, college students move in and retirees go to Florida.

"Still, Boston stays near 600,000 and Providence stays near 150,000 and knowing these estimated numbers tells us a lot about these two places."

"Yeah, Boston is a lot bigger," said Diana, "it has subways and really tall buildings."

"And Fenway Park," added Jonah.

"And the Science Museum," said Rebecca.

"I don't think we can design a city that big," said Thomas.

Evan nodded and said, "Let's make it more like the size of Providence."

"Or even smaller," said Philip. "Instead of 150,000 people, lets make it 100,000 people."

From that number, the mathematical structure of our city began to take shape. Using the proportion of children to adults in the class families, we calculated the likely number of children and teenagers and, using our figures for how many children it takes to support a video arcade, determined that our city could support three such establishments. Abe and William were happy. They seemed to have forgotten the wish for a video arcade in every neighborhood and appeared gratified that we would have arcades in three of our eight neighborhoods.

We calculated the number of schools and developed neighborhoods with a mix of apartment complexes and single family houses. We figured out how many jobs would be needed and imagined local businesses such as grocery stores in each neighborhood and downtown businesses with many employees.

Big sheets of paper were used to sketch maps and we agreed on transportation systems, and a long serpentine river and a lake that connected lobes of residential areas. By the time we moved onto drawing detailed maps the mood was eager and intense. Everyone was assigned a section of the city, and, drawing to our agreed upon scale, each student sketched homes, roads, schools, and businesses. Ultimately, we would produce a huge map that covered our entire hallway bulletin board.

One day, while everyone was immersed in mapmaking, Jonah raised his hand.

"We forgot something," he said. "A homeless shelter."

I smiled. "This city isn't going to need a homeless shelter," I said, "because there will be no homeless people. That is the beauty of a planned city," I continued confidently. "It will be organized so that everyone has a home."

"Get real Mrs. Allsup!" Ariana interjected, "You might not think there will be homeless people, but there will be."

"I see what you mean," I said. "The people who designed Brasilia imagined that their city would be perfect and that nobody would live in poverty. But, it all didn't go as planned and the city grew more quickly than expected and lots of people lived in poverty outside the city. So you are right that sometimes the best planning doesn't work. But, still, I would like to think that planners had learned something since Brasilia and that, if we made such a new city today, we would find a way for everyone to have a good home."

We might have let this rest, let it go for now as an impasse. But then Reesa spoke. Her voice was soft, but everyone heard her short sentence.

"I was homeless once."

Thomas and Evan had been drawing. They stopped and looked at Reesa. The room was very quiet.

She continued, "It was when I was really little. Instead of a shelter, we had to live in a motel. And there was no kitchen and it was really small."

The room was quiet. Pencils were down. This wasn't faceless homelessness. It was Reesa. It was a place for Reesa to live, baby Reesa when she was really little. And it wasn't necessarily true that in our city she would have a good home. And a shelter is better than no home at all.

The faces looking at me did not hold a question about whether our city would have a homeless shelter. It was a demand, a moral imperative.

It was my turn to feel a sense of awe, to be profoundly moved by the sense of social justice that lived in my class, by the fact that their definition of magnificence in a city would not be about tall buildings, an amazing zoo or a fast subway but by the availability of a place to live just in case someone had no home at all.

"You are right," I said. "We will have a homeless shelter. But, how will the math work? How will we pay for it?"

Abe spoke up right away. "I know," he said, with a spark in his eyes that signaled another important proclamation, one that would be met with universal approval, "we will use the profits from the video arcades!"

24

Destiny

TODAY IS THE DAY that I will tell the class. I have already told their parents. They had promised not to tell their children themselves, promised to let me bring them the news. They will be waiting at the door at the end of the day, knowing that the news is fresh, ready to support their children's unexpected transition. My fellow teachers know it too; they have been part of the careful planning and are ready for the word to move from class to class during recess the next morning.

Today, I will tell them. But not until the end of the day. Now, early at school, I sit at my desk, turn my chair to face the Bourne Bridge and remember the night when this decision came to me, unexpected on the highway, the highway that begins at the graceful curve of the silver bridge, and goes north toward New Hampshire.

I remember feeling the decision that night before I made it, feeling something unexpected and not knowing what to make of it.

I had been driving north to pick up Nora. Her headaches had exploded into an endless nightmare, each episode three days of agony followed by two days of exhaustion. One or two or three days later it would all begin again with the clouded vision that signals a new migraine cycle.

We had decided that she would leave boarding school, where

dormitory life was too loud to allow her to sleep off the pain, and that she would come home to stay.

It was meant to be my last trip north, but, strangely, I had felt it was not an ending, but a beginning, that we were not moving away from New Hampshire, but toward it. I remembered being puzzled by the strength of this inexplicable sensation that I was being pulled north to stay, and just listening to this feeling for awhile, the feeling I should not be having.

Driving in that late autumn night, I had reflected on my hurried phone conversation with Geoff on my way out the door. "My boss says I can mostly work from home," he had said. There had been no time for a conversation about this. I didn't know why he had said it. I supposed it had something to do with Nora being home so much. No doubt he thought, as I did, that it would be better if Nora did not have to spend so much time alone. I wondered how he would find space for all his equipment, computers, oscilloscopes, tall ocean instruments, and boxes of electronic parts in our little house on Cape Cod.

But, then, being pulled to the North by some unknown force, I realized that Geoff had meant something else, the unthinkable, but obvious. We could move to New Hampshire. Nora could go back to the Waldorf high school as a day student. She could live in a quiet home, rather than a loud dormitory. She would be able to sleep off her headaches. She clearly needed the daily encouragement of parents to face such a debilitating illness. We would be able to support her in her medical journey.

I could finish this year with my class. Nora could do another spring semester at the community college. We could move in the summer and she could repeat a grade.

This was not the life I had ever imagined, a life that required that I leave my class, leave our school, leave Cape Cod. Communion with tides, sea scented morning fog, ever-present gulls and the traditions of all seafaring folk, all this was part of my essence. I had felt that it was not only my destiny to teach, but to teach in this place, to draw my students into an understanding of this lowland, saltwater peninsula. I had never imagined a life in the mountains rather than by the sea. But, there on the highway, traveling north, I knew suddenly and surely it was the life we had to choose for Nora's sake.

At that moment, I had been like Rama. Accepting a move to the hill country of southern New Hampshire as the best choice for our family would not takes weeks of agonizing discussion. I knew it would be our direction then and there. Nora, who had experienced three class teachers in her journey through our school, and who had grieved at each departure, would say, "But Mom, you can't leave your class." And I would answer, "I have to. I never thought that anything could stop me from finishing the eight years with my class. But, then, I never imagined that you would be so sick. Right now it is time to put you first. You need to stay in school and you need your home to be near your school. I will be sad to leave my class, but they can get a new teacher. You can't get a new Mom."

Now I sit in my empty classroom, looking at the road north that begins at the silver bridge. Sounds in the hallway alert me to my first arrivals. I shake hands with Jonah, then Evan. We chat about the day. I move into my early morning dance between writing on the blackboard and greeting each student. I am aware of the sense of comfort we all have with each other, of the feelings of trust and continuity that have grown over more than five years.

I wonder if tomorrow morning will feel like this or whether my kids will already be taking a small step away, beginning the unconscious process of distancing themselves from me so they would be ready for that last goodbye in June. All day, up to the last period, which I have saved for my announcement, I watch my kids and savor the sense that they are still mine.

Once, in the early years of our school, an advisor told us that we might not be ready to be a full eight grade school, that we should consider stopping after fifth grade. It is a good time for a transition, he had said, at that age when children have reached a high level of competence, when they have attained a pinnacle of physical grace, in that last year before the dawning of puberty.

I had been watching the difference between fifth and sixth graders and I could see what he had meant. The fifth graders, ten-year-olds nearing eleven, appeared free. They were tall and lithe. In contrast, my four sixth graders and Roland, my oldest fifth grader, three boys and two girls, eleven-year-olds nearing twelve, had broader shoulders and a gait that seems to anchor them more firmly to the earth.

I knew already that the older class would disband and move on to other schools. Rebecca and Andy would go to the prep school that Nora had left due to her illness. William would return to public school. Helen's family had already been planning to move to another state. I knew too that most of the fifth grade would stay.

At the end of the day I say, "I saved some time before closing to have a conversation about something important." I ask them to take their chairs and make a circle. We sit in a cozy group and I start to talk about Rama.

We had long since finished our study of India and moved on to Mesopotamia, Egypt, and Greece, so the class looks at me curiously. Why are we talking about Rama again, they wonder.

They are too polite to say this aloud, but I can hear it. I can hear so much of what they don't say. I have spent almost six years learning to understand this silence. Their new teacher will not read this class so deeply for some time. It is this understanding that is being sacrificed in making this choice.

Rama had to give up the idea that he would become king. I am giving up more.

Today I need Rama. The class needs Rama. We all need his message that, if we are enlightened, we will accept our destiny cheerfully.

I ask them to tell me the beginning of the story one more time. Bit by bit, the pieces come together, the plan for Rama's kingship, the father's commitment to the stepmother to grant any wish, the stepmother's delayed and unexpected request, a prior commitment that turned out to be a bigger commitment than anticipated, the father's unenlightened response, Rama's calm and enlightened reaction to the news that he will not become king, Rama's banishment and his eventual return.

The class humors me with the telling of this already over-considered story. Then I begin.

"Rama found that life does not always move along as we expect it. He was an enlightened being and so he was able to accept the unexpected events in his life with an amazing cheerfulness.

"As you all know I have had unexpected things happen in my life over the last couple of years. Nora has been sick with lots of serious headaches, and she had to leave boarding school in New Hampshire. It was too hard for her to live in a dormitory while she was so sick.

"It meant a lot to her to be at that school and we want to keep her there. But she is too sick to live in a dormitory, so we have had to make a very difficult decision. We have decided to move to New Hampshire so she can live at home and go to school. And that means that you and I, like Rama, are going to face a future very different than what we had expected for many years. I always thought I would teach you through eighth grade. But now I have to tell you that destiny has taken me in another direction."

It is quiet while I let this sink in.

There is much to read in this silence. Rebecca's stoic surprise. My basketball boys each pulling into a separate, deep place. Reesa's eyes filling with tears.

"It means you will have a different teacher next year. I told the other teachers as early as I could so there would be time to look for a great teacher.

"This is hard for me too. I love all of you and will miss you so much. But I have been trying to think like Rama and not get too sad. After the end of this school year, I will not see you everyday, but you will still be important to me. We all knew that at eighth grade I would change from being your teacher to being your friend. Now this will happen sooner than we expected."

I answered a few questions and then we ended the day with our usual closing verse.

Then, it was time to shake hands and turn the class over to their waiting parents. It was in that second, standing between the children and their parents, that I suddenly felt an abiding connection. Shaking each child's hand, I felt enmeshed in a community that was too strong, too much a part of us to go away. I would no longer teach these children day after day, year after year, but I would love them forever.

25

Main Lessons

It is absolutely essential that before we think, before we so much as begin
to set our thinking in motion, we experience the condition of wonder.
—Rudolf Steiner

USUALLY I was the one with chalk in my hand, facing my fifth and sixth graders, speaking while listening, drawing while watching students draw, thinking while wondering about each child's thoughts.

But, today, sitting in the back of the room near the tall windows, I watched another teacher about to begin a lesson. Mr. DuFord, a visiting teacher who was applying for my job, picked up a piece of chalk and walked to the front of the room. I watched my students too. Helen leaned over and whispered to Rebecca. Jonah tipped his chair back and looked out the window. William's head nodded to the rhythm of an imagined rap beat.

Then I saw beyond what I was seeing. I saw a snow fort built of atom-like spheres. I saw Reesa dancing in the autumn leaves. I saw smiling Marc in his red wheelchair, a white kitten hanging from the edge of a box, children nailing shingles onto a playhouse, Rebecca skating backwards and Roland inching along the boards, children running around a campfire and William sinking into his chair, drinking in the applause of his classmates.

I saw, too, a taut but delicate strand of spider's web suspended in midair and I remembered knowing that the filaments that held up the strand must be invisible, yet real, and I remembered seeking, ever seeking, invisible elements that would support my teaching.

Now my students looked expectantly at another teacher. Soon they would have another teacher every day.

There was once a time when they could not read or write, add or subtract. When they did not know the meaning of continental divide, metamorphosis or photosynthesis. When they had never heard of Socrates, Governor Bradford, or Mother Theresa. Now they knew something of all of this.

Mr. DuFord, a professional artist new to teaching, held up a picture of Alexander the Great. He taped it to the blackboard and said, "I want you to forget that this is a picture of a man and a horse. Instead, just look for shapes. Totally forget the details. Look for the biggest shapes you can find. For instance, look at this area. You could see the shape of the shield and the shape of the arm as two separate areas. But I want you to see something bigger. Can you look at that area and see a bigger shape?"

Evan raised his hand.

"Come up to the board and show us." Evan gripped the chalk and formed a squarish shape.

"Nice job," Mr. DuFord smiled at Evan as he turned to go back to his seat.

Then he picked up the chalk and continued Evan's work. "The classical artists all worked like this. They began with large shapes, and then they layered smaller shapes on top of the larger ones. Bit by bit, these layers grew into a drawing or a painting. This approach is what makes a scene have depth, makes it seem so real you could walk right into it."

"So, find your crayons and begin to draw the largest shapes you can find. It's fine, in fact it's good, if they overlap. The main thing to remember is to stay with the big shapes as long as you can."

Eyes traveled from blackboard to paper, up to the board, back

to the paper. Reesa squinted, Thomas frowned, Jonah raised his left
hand to his chin and tipped his head to the right.

I drank in their mood of concentration, their intense connection
with their work. And, again, I saw beyond what I was seeing, felt
beyond what I was feeling. I remembered little children captivated
by falling leaves, wide eyes reacting to a suspenseful story, provocative
smiles that gave levity to our math games, shared smiles on a hike in
the woods, indignant groaning as I stopped mid-story and said, "We
will finish this tomorrow."

I saw that, as a teacher, I had taught more than facts, more than
math processes, more than spelling, more than grammar.

I listened to the gentle scraping of crayons, the creaking of wood-
en chairs and, for just a moment, I let go. I let go of evaluating this
teaching applicant, let go of tuning into the children, let go of my
musings. I drifted with the sounds of the school—solitary footsteps
in the hallway, laughter from the room next-door, far-off sounds of
children singing.

My mind drifted, drifted to a small office at the end of my student days, just before I began my life as a teacher. There, one of my
teachers had told me I was too much in my head.

I didn't understand her words then, but I did now. She had been
right of course. I did start out too much in my head. Maybe we all
do. Maybe the essence of our crisis in raising children is that we are
convinced that the work of teachers and parents is mostly centered in
thinking, that we do not know deeply enough that in order to truly
support children, our work must begin in the heart.

Now I focused again on Mr. DuFord and I saw that he was, without realizing it, speaking about a great truth that transcended this
art lesson. The main thing Mr. DuFord wanted the children to perceive as they worked on their drawings was that beginning with large

defining forms and working, layer by layer, toward the smaller details would give the drawing a sense of balance and proportion, would make it feel right and beautiful. I remembered that in teacher training we had been offered similar advice about teaching from the whole to the parts—to, for instance, speak the whole poem to a class before helping them memorize it line by line.

I saw that in so many tasks, there is a tendency to jump too soon to the details, to the lines of the poem, to the small elements in a drawing. Mr. DuFord's statement about beginning with the contextual and staying with it as long as possible could be a guiding principle for the future of education not just in individual classrooms, but in the way we look at the entire endeavor. Teaching and parenting will feel right and beautiful when we start with the monumental work of enriching children by supporting wonder, curiosity, and a love for the world and for each other. This is the context for holding the smaller elements—facts, skills, and general knowledge.

"Let's put our crayons down for a moment to see what we have drawn."

Mr. DuFord leaned over Reesa's drawing. "Yes, you have the idea. This is coming along quite well."

He moved from student to student, making quick comments on each drawing, "Good."

"Nice."

"I like the way you are taking your time."

And then he addressed the whole class, "Before we go back to our work, I have a question for you. What is the biggest shape in your drawing?"

Thomas raised his hand and said, "The area with the horse."

Mr. DuFord nodded and tilted his head in a way that said,"This is good, but I am looking for something else."

Philip slowly raised his hand.

"Yes?" asked Mr. DuFord.

"It's the whole picture of Alexander and the horse. It makes a big shape almost like a triangle on the page."

Mr. DuFord grinned and said, "That's what I hoped you'd see." He paused. "But there's still something else. Something even bigger."

Rebecca and Helen turned to each other and shrugged. Ariana raised her hand. "Is it the part that doesn't have any picture at all?"

"Show me what you mean."

She shrugged, walked to the board and gestured tentatively toward the area above and around Alexander and his horse.

"Yes!" exclaimed Mr. DuFord."That's it! The biggest shape is what we often ignore, the background."

Marc, who had grown fond of big philosophical questions, smiled as Mr. DuFord posed this interesting concept, that it is the background, the part we don't usually notice, that is an important part of the picture.

I smiled too. I thought about the background of our years together as a class, the part we did not create together, the part that was given—the children's evolving lives outside of school, my own life with its joys and challenges, the ships gliding by on the canal, the deep wisdom of ancient legends, and, above all, the world of the spirit, so often sensed and not so often understood. The tapestry I wove with the children, the foreground of their growing knowledge and skills was supported by a larger mid-ground of their developing inner lives, their character, and all of it was woven into this background fabric. This great background shape stood over and around the mid-ground and the foreground, but also lay behind it so that it shone through the luminous colors of our days.

Part of the background reality that supported this art lesson was the silent hallway outside our door. Now, exuberant voices and the metallic clanging of lockers in the hall told us it was time to move to the next class.

Mr. DuFord said, "It looks like it is time to finish up. You have all made a good start. Perhaps Mrs. Allsup can find time for you to finish your drawings."

I stood and joined my colleague in the front of the room. I assured the class that they would have a chance to finish their drawings. Then I shook his hand and thanked him for teaching the lesson. I raised my eyebrows and nodded at the class. They knew this to be their cue. "Thank you, Mr. DuFord," they recited in unison. They cleared their desks and broke into happy chatting as they filed out the door.

I did not know at that moment that Mr. DuFord would not be the teacher who would carry my class into the future. But, I did know that whether or not he had a destiny with my children, he had brought me an important lesson.

"I'm on my way to teach writing in the seventh grade," I told him as I gathered books and papers from my desk. "But I'll see you after school at your interview." I walked to the door, then turned.

"I think the class learned something from your lesson today. I know I did. I like what you said, 'Stay with the big shapes as long as you can.'"

I like to live with good questions, to seek answers and to modify these answers over months and years. I left Mr. DuFord's art class with questions that have been worth living with for a very long time. As teachers and as parents, what does it mean, to stay with the big shapes as long as we can? What is the context that is worth holding continually in our hearts and minds, worth staying with as long as we can?

Long ago, in first grade, we began our journey together with a mood of innocent wonder, a time of openness to the world that was infused with magic and fueled by imagination. If our work as a class had been a drawing, this would have been the biggest shape, the open wonder of the young child. By third grade we had moved into a time when wonder was rooted in reality. Now the metaphorical drawing would include a new, translucent layer of eager interest, a new sort of grounded wonder brightened by the layer of innocent awe that had preceded it.

Whether, sparked by the imagination or by verifiable truth, wonder is the stem cell of human character. It contains a forward-looking hopeful openness that can grow into reverence, love, an eagerness for learning, and a capacity for work. Wonder has a way of propelling us toward all that is good and positive. It also transforms into essential elements of the human character—confidence, curiosity, attention, listening, resilience, gratitude, perspective, respect, nurturing, responsibility, inquiry, balance, insight, hope, friendship, freedom, experience, healing, and compassion. All of these are deep layers in our drawing. We had found time, made time, to weave these great, background shapes into our essence as a class, into the soul of each child. For who we are and what we become in childhood is the big shape that anchors a life.

This ongoing inner work, the deep layers of our drawing, had not distracted us from our details: times tables, poetry recitations, book discussions, fractions, Greek history, the study of botany, geometry, and so much more. Rather, nurturing wonder as a context for learning had made our years real, made our school days something my kids and I wanted to walk into each morning. The main thing we had remembered was to stay with the big shapes as long as we could.

26

Love

Receive the child in reverence, educate the child in love, let the child go in freedom.
—Rudolf Steiner

FINALLY, I had decided what to do with the eighth grade box.

Alone in the classroom, I pulled the original box off the high closet shelf. Then I tugged at the second and third boxes full of the class memorabilia that would not fit in the first box. A lower shelf held six 4-foot-long cotton scrolls. These I rolled onto my forearms and carried to a child's desk.

First grade gnomes, a construction blueprint for the small house we built in third grade, playbills from all of our plays, notes from parents, "Please allow Mark to go home with Evan today." The key to the map of the city we designed, the sword of light from our second grade play, many years of verses by Saint Nicholas. All of this I unloaded into a disorganized pile on my desk.

I had decided that we would end our time together with an auction, an auction of all of this stuff, these bits of paper and cloth, wood and words, echoes of our moments together. It would be a way to honor our memories in a way that I hoped would elicit laughter rather than tears. Tonight I would make the play money I planned to distribute to the class, five hundred "Waldorf dollars" for each child.

One at a time, I carried items to the hall and pinned them to the large bulletin board where we had recently posted the map of our city, complete with a homeless shelter. Then, inside the classroom, I unrolled the tapestries we had painted in third grade, each representing a day from the Old Testament story of creation. Five of these I hung around the room.

The large cloth painting that represented the fifth day of Biblical creation showed a dark blue breaching whale, hovering gulls, and a green-blue sea. Now, on the verge of our move to the hill country of New Hampshire, I wished I could hold on to the sea, to my Cape Cod kids, who like me, had sand in their shoes and the screech of gulls echoing in their dreams. I would ask the class if they minded if I kept this painting.

It was all done now except for the clean up, just the empty boxes to put away. Lifting the original eighth grade box to put it back in the closet, I heard a faint thump. A last item had slid out from under a bottom flap. It was a chewed, green pencil with a piece of paper wrapped around it and secured with a rubber band. Recognizing the item that had caused a big squabble in second grade, I sat down at my desk and, sliding off the elastic, uncurled the paper. It said "Reesa and Jonah disagreed about who owned this pencil in second grade."

I didn't take this item to the wall of memories. Instead, I rewrapped it and put it in my top desk drawer. The pencil would not go on display; I would surprise the class with it. I smiled, looking forward to that moment when, after more than four years, Jonah and Reesa would bring their argument to a close by turning to each other and, laughing, say something like "you can have that old thing. It probably wasn't mine anyway."

Now I was done, ready for our last morning together, a half-day of school when we would say our goodbyes. I looked again at the wall of memories.

This could have been a time for tears. I felt them lurking, held back by an invisible dam. My kids certainly knew that I cried at sad stories, at unexpected moments of academic breakthroughs, at almost anything that was profound or deep. And, I knew that my watery nature meant that I had to work hard, exceptionally hard, to stay on Rama's path through the day ahead. For, if the dam broke now, I was not convinced that I could repair it by morning.

The tears would come, but not yet. I would hold them back until after the final all-school assembly, after the auction and the goodbye hugs and handshakes at the classroom door, after the goodbye party at Evan's house. They would come the following day, when I was expected back at school for a day of teacher's meetings.

I would not be anything like Rama on that day when I was too distraught to go to the meetings. Between sobs, I would think about the fact that, all over the world, fifth and sixth grade students bid farewell to teachers who shed no tears, who said simple goodbyes and looked forward to a summer with some rest and new group of kids in the fall. And I would wonder if, somehow, it made a difference, an important difference, to my students that I loved them.

With only an hour left in our time together, we pushed the desks back to the windows and lined up chairs in rows facing the door. My kids, who had already surveyed each item on display, took one last look.

By the time all were seated, Waldorf dollars in hand, I could see that this was actually going to work. I could see it in their upright postures, in their eyes. I knew this look. It was like the anticipation that preceded the second, concluding day of a captivating story. It was the face of an older child's version of wonder, a look that was different for each person and showed a bit of their character.

My request to keep the whale tapestry as my memento was met with gracious nods.

Then we were off.

"How much will you bid for this gnome from first grade? Do I see five dollars? Thank you Diana. Ten from Helen. Fifteen from Ariana." The bidding went back and forth between all the girls. All the girls except for Rebecca put in a bid on the big fuzzy gnome that had been a classroom friend in our first years together. When we reached one hundred pretend dollars the bidding stopped. Arianna had offered this high bid. She had joined the class just this year and had no memories of cradling this doll in first grade. Maybe, I thought, she had not spent enough time with gnome dolls in her previous school. I handed her the big red gnome.

We continued like this through play props, play bills, classroom toys, drawings and verses on colorful paper. I looked at my watch. I could see this was going to take more time than I had thought. I began bundling things together. A playbill with a prop from the play, a handful of parent notes.

The blueprints of our third grade house were bundled in a set of two, a larger print and a smaller one. These drawings were wildly popular and almost everyone (except Rebecca, who had not placed any bids and still had every penny of her five hundred Waldorf dollars) put in a bid on these accurate blue images that had been drawn by Philip's father. Andy ultimately put in the final bid and won the prints for $350, our highest price for any item so far. He accepted the prints with a big grin and an announcement. "Now I'm broke. I spent all of it."

So, five minutes later when I held up a fourth grade playbill, I was surprised when Andy raised his hand and called out, "Ten dollars!"

"Hold everything," I said. "Andy, didn't you spend all your money?"

"I did," he laughed. "But, I sold the small blueprint to Thomas for $50, so I made a profit." We all joined Andy in his mirth. As I picked up another item, I reflected on how appropriate it was that Andy, a sixth grade student who had studied business math this year, had come up with the ingenious plan to resell items for profit.

Now I unrolled the big fabric paintings, one for each day of the Biblical creation. "Many of you remember painting these in small groups in third grade. And you remember our presentation when we recited the words from the Old Testament about the creation and raised these one at a time in front of the windows while singing. These paintings are very special and I considered not putting them in the auction. But, in the end, I realized that great art is sold in auctions everyday. So, take a moment to admire these and then we will start the bidding."

Who will give me one hundred dollars for this painting that represents the first day of creation in the Bible? I pointed at the dark bordered square of cloth with a bright tumbling center of light. Everyone seemed willing to spend all their remaining money for this painting, everyone except for Rebecca, the only person who still clutched five hundred Waldorf dollars. Thomas had bought the resold blueprints, but not much else, so he had enough to outbid everyone for the hazy pastel painting in which "the waters are divided from the waters" in the second day of creation.

When I pointed to the painting representing the third day of creation, with its tall pine tree shooting up amid the grass by a purple-blue sea, I saw Rebecca brighten. "Do I have an opening bid?" I asked. Rebecca raised her hand and said calmly, "Five hundred dollars."

I didn't have to wait for more bids. I knew Rebecca, who, like Andy, had studied business math, had been the only one to save all of her money.

I heard a gasp as I said, "Gone for five hundred dollars."

The gasp was answered by the hushed voice of a classmate, "She never spent any money."

Soon the rest of the large cloth paintings were sold and it appeared that everything was gone. A soft chatter filled the room, "What did you get?"

"Did you spend all your money?"

"I still have fifty dollars left."

"I have one hundred."

I interrupted these conversations saying, "We have one more thing. It's something small and it's here in my desk drawer."

The class was quiet as I held up the chewed green pencil wrapped with a piece of paper secured by an elastic band.

"I wonder if some of you remember this." I slid the elastic off the pencil, unrolled the paper and read, "Reesa and Jonah disagreed about who owned this pencil in second grade."

"I remember that," said Philip. "Me too." said Evan. A rumble of recognition and confusion swept though the room. I reminded Helen and Marc that they were at different schools during that year and told them and our newcomers about the impasse that had led to my putting the contested pencil in the eighth grade box.

"We put this in the box in second grade and I said that we would take it out in eighth grade. We didn't make it to eighth grade together, but I think that enough time has gone by that you both know how silly it was to fight over a pencil, a short, chewed up pencil at that."

This was the moment when Reesa or Jonah was supposed to say, "Yeah, you can have that old thing. I don't want a chewed up pencil."

But, instead, Reesa said, "I will bid twenty."

Jonah countered with a spirited, "I've got thirty."

Then, all at once, everyone who had money left jumped into a chaotic, noisy, disorganized bidding melee, all for a chewed up green pencil.

I held up my hand and called out, "Quiet."

"I don't get it," I said. "This is a sad looking pencil. I thought, after all these years, Jonah and Reesa would each offer it to the other one and say they were sorry for fighting over it. But, instead, everyone wants it and, in a way, they are still fighting over it, you are all fighting over it."

My kids laughed as I said this, and, in exaggerated, whining imitations of their second grade voices, called out, "But I want it."

"No, it should be mine."

"I wasn't here in second grade, so I think I should have it."

I smiled as I saw that they had learned this lesson about minor disagreements long ago, and that now we were exploring a new sort of lesson, one about the value of our memories. Their historic squabbles were now something to remember fondly. The chewed up green pencil itself had become an icon, the last cherished item in our auction, a symbol of our years together, a tangible reflection of our memories. It had been preserved because of its role in a historic battle, a small battle that was now a humorous part of our wonder years.

The room was charged with energy as I resumed the bidding. Neither Jonah nor Reesa, who were both low on money, ended up with the pencil. It did not matter much who ended up with it, for we went away with one last lesson: It is not the pencil itself. Nor is it the object, the data, the facts or the lesson content, but our relationship to these that makes them worth having, worth knowing.

The auction had taken us past the usual dismissal time. Parents could be heard outside the door. I thought about giving a short goodbye speech. But then I saw that this might dampen the mood, might erase the smiling sense of fulfillment that permeated the classroom as my class clutched evidence of our years together. So, I moved us into the usual closing, a group recitation of a poem.

Then, opening the door to a hall full of parents, I hugged each child and said a fond goodbye.

"Look, Mom, look what I got!" Children handed their hauls to moms and dads. Jeremy smiled through the tears that ran down his face. Long ago, he had let go of a need for frequent approval and replaced it with deep connections to me, to his classmates and to his work.

My children left with their arms full of wonderful memories, focused, for the most part, not on what had been lost, but on what they had gained.

REFLECTIONS

27

School as it Should Be

Everything that is really great and inspiring is created by the individual who can labor in freedom.
—Albert Einstein

MY STUDENTS WERE ELEVEN AND TWELVE years old in 1997, the year we auctioned off our memories. In 2015, as I completed my account of our years together, they stood at twenty-nine and thirty years of age, industrious young adults pursuing careers, nurturing families, improving their communities. Nora had made true the prediction of one of her doctors by growing out of her illness during her twenties. As for myself, after shepherding three additional classes, I enjoyed semi-retirement as a part-time gardening teacher, mentor of new teachers and writer of books for children.

As I look back on my my time as a class teacher, the faces of the children I taught, my excitement about bringing lessons to my classes and evanescent and heartwarming moments with my students dance in my memory. My twenty-two years as a class teacher were good from beginning to end. However, my teaching experience stands in contrast to that of thousands of public school teachers who have had their professional judgment and creative freedom increasingly curtailed over the past two decades.

Almost every week I read a resignation letter from an experienced public school teacher who details how his or her classroom experience went from good to bad to worse. Here is a compelling excerpt from such a letter written by David Xirau who resigned from public school teaching in Massachusetts in January of 2015:

> Authentic teaching is done free of the restrictive standards, unattainable objectives, and insanely burdensome administrative minutiae that are imposed upon us every day. [...]

> What is the real cost of this extra work? Who is paying the price when our minds and energy are devoted to endless testing, development of standards and objectives, rubrics, measurement, results, analysis, DDMs, improvement plans, PLCs, "Smart" goals, evidence collecting, percentages, alignments, core curriculum, cross curriculum, accommodations, modifications, incessant IEP paperwork, meetings, data, data, data, and more data? Read the list again!! Where is the pedagogy? When do we get to teach?

> Students need to be taught, not analyzed. They are human beings, not an experiment, not parts of a machine coming off of an assembly line. My students need and deserve my full attention, something I cannot give under the current circumstances.

When I began teaching, educators in both public and private schools were expected to bring their own judgment and their creative energies to their students. But, today, as Mr. Xirau lamented in his resignation letter, requirements related to rigid curricula and narrow standards, and a sense of anxiety about the need to prepare students for the next high stakes test, have left little or no time to focus on the care of specific children or a class as a whole. Teachers in many public schools are not allowed to develop their own engaging lessons or tailor that lesson for the needs of a class or an individual. Nor are they allowed to stray from the required lesson plan to welcome an unplanned discussion.

Indeed, if my classroom had been in a typical public school in recent years, the most transformative moments we experienced during our six-year journey might have been seen by my superiors as evidence of noncompliance with the state and federal rules that now direct the classroom lives of most teachers and their students.

Most teachers today would not feel it was their call to create a special lesson about Tom Thumb to support a positive self-image in a first grader. In schools where teachers are constrained by rubrics, scripted lessons, and textbook-centered lesson plans, a ten minute segue devoted to healing a rift over a pencil would not be sanctioned. Teachers aren't free to seize opportunities to spark wonder and harness engagement. In many schools today, teachers lack permission to bring a kitten to school, accept a student initiative of a race to test methods for adding fractions, build a playhouse, spend a morning walking through the spring woods, or develop number sense by helping students come up with their own design for a city in which video arcades fund homeless shelters. What is lost is that sense of spontaneity and joy that makes learning feel natural and unforced.

A teacher who works in freedom develops a consciousness that is, at times, akin to the intuitive perspective of an artist. Waiting by the closed door at the end of recess for Reesa. Feeling the urgency of the class's first argument and quietly letting it happen. Deciding on the spot to take my lesson about rivers outside to the sandbox. Recasting the planned story of Demosthenes mid-lesson to prolong the unexpected engagement of a disaffected child. Looking back, I am grateful to have worked in a school where I was not only allowed to rely on my intuition and judgment, but was actively encouraged to develop the deep connections with my students that would make my perception worthwhile.

Mr. DuFord told my students that classical painters started with the big shapes and stayed with them for as long as they could, working on details only after the broad geometry of the painting was well established. Building the broad geometry of the self is the central task of childhood. This configuration of the inner child becomes the guiding gesture of the future adult. Narrow standards should not come first. Tests should not come first. Nurturing this broad geometry of the self, the robust physical and psychological health of each individual child, must be recognized as the first task of teachers. This is the big shape, the guiding form, for us to stay with as long as we can.

Someday, I hope to read to read an uplifting classroom memoir about creative freedom in teaching that is set in a public school. Meanwhile, there is much that Waldorf education can offer to those re-envisioning public education.

A casual visitor to any grade one through eight Waldorf school might notice first graders knitting bright rainbow scarves. The visitor might hear a cacophony of string instruments tuning before class, the scraping of chisels in the woodwork room, a lilting song in harmony, a voice bellowing in Shakespearean anger as part of drama rehearsal. A peek through a door might show children jumping rope while reciting a times table or drawing in the lesson books they create for themselves instead of using textbooks. A glance out the window is likely to reveal children building a fort in the woods or working in a garden. The visitor sees tools everywhere. Colored pencils, shovels, violins, crochet hooks, sewing machines, jump ropes, and chisels are wielded by students developing the skills of musicians, artists, gardeners, woodworkers, and hand crafters.

Such a casual visitor can easily identify obvious ways in which the Waldorf approach is different from methods used in most schools: the use of simple hand tools in elementary school before the introduction of the complex tool of the sewing machine in middle school and computers in late middle school and high school; the continuity of teachers shepherding a class for multiple years; the two hour main lesson at the start of the day; the lack of textbooks and the student creation of colorful, illustrated books that document learning. All of these visible elements are proven and ready to be borrowed by public schools, but none are more important than the invisible thread of caring, creative freedom in teaching that runs through this memoir. This is the vital essence of education that has been sucked out of most schools today and what we must strive, above all, to bring back.

Acknowledgements

When it takes fifteen years to write a book, there is a good chance that your literary agent will retire long before the last chapter is written. I am most grateful to Nina Ryan for her belief in this project during its inception and her advice in shaping the book. I tried to follow her advice to "let the children speak." I send thanks as well to the many literary agents who graciously turned me down while offering useful, free advice.

My master's thesis at Antioch University included an early version of about half of this book. Torin Finser and Arthur Auer provided support and guidance in the early stages of writing and in the early stages of my teaching career and for this I am most grateful.

Many thanks to David Xirau for allowing me to quote part of his resignation letter.

I am profoundly grateful to the late Ruth Finser who read and edited an early version of the manuscript and offered key ideas for the introduction.

I send heartfelt appreciation to Patrice Maynard for writing the foreword.

Thank you to the staff at SteinerBooks, especially John Scott Legg.

Many colleagues, friends and family members read all or part of the manuscript and offered encouragement and editorial help. You guys kept me going on this project: Bobbi Bailin, Beverly Thompson Gardner, Bob Opaluch, Jeanne Wescott, Alan Gardner (who read the manuscript on a ship in the middle of the Pacific Ocean), Ben Allsup, Erica Szuplat, Fran Denoncourt, Nadine Bender Worstell, Cheryl Twombly, Peg Szuplat, Mary Collins, Ted Curtin, Goldie and Gilbert Gillis and Ieeda Rico. Two kind friends helped develop the Indiegogo campaign. Robert

Leaver brought insighful comments to the written part and Rhonwen Churchill created the video.

I am in awe of my colleagues at the Waldorf School of Cape Cod and at Waldorf schools around the globe who make their schools thrive, often in an environment of meager political and financial support. I am hoping that this book showcases your craft and inspires school systems in the public sector to trust teachers to do their most important work in freedom. I am most grateful to be among your ranks.

My students and their parents have been my best teachers. I am thankful for the privilege of being involved in their lives.

Special thanks to our daughter, Nora Allsup Gardner, for allowing me to share her teenage health challenges.

I could not imagine a more supportive spouse for my endeavors as a teacher and a writer. My husband Geoff kept my computers going, edited each chapter more than once, took on more than his share of housekeeping, and never complained about any of it, even my disappearing acts during our summer vacations.

Kim Allsup's childhood wonder years inspired her first career as an environmentalist and her second career as a Waldorf teacher. She was the founding staff member of the Buzzard Bay Coalition and a founding parent of the Waldorf School of Cape Cod. A graduate of Brown University and Antioch University (M.Ed), she served as a Waldorf class teacher, on Cape Cod and at the Pine Hill Waldorf School, for 22 years. She is currently a writer, an advisor to teachers, and a gardening teacher pioneering the use of school sunhouses. She lives on Cape Cod with her husband. Read her blog about the art of helping children grow at ChildrenGrowing.com.